Preaching Ethically

Preaching Ethically

*Being True to the Gospel, the
Congregation, and Yourself*

Ronald D. Sisk

THE
ALBAN
INSTITUTE

Herndon, Virginia
www.alban.org

The Alban Institute
2121 Cooperative Way, Suite 100
Herndon, VA 20171-5370

Unless otherwise noted, all Scripture quotations are from the New Revised Standard Version of the Bible, copyright © 1989, Division of Christian Education of the National Council of the Churches of Christ in the United States of America, and are used by permission.

Cover design by Tobias Becker.

Library of Congress Cataloging-in-Publication Data

Sisk, Ronald D.
  Preaching ethically : being true to the gospel, the congregation, and yourself / Ronald D. Sisk.
      p. cm. — (The vital worship, healthy congregations series)
  Includes bibliographical references.
  ISBN 978-1-56699-361-6
  1. Preaching. 2. Integrity—Religious aspects—Christianity. I. Title.

BV4211.3.S57 2007
251—dc22
                                          2007045799

12   11   10   09   08   VG   1   2   3   4   5

Contents

Editor's Foreword

Healthy Congregations

Christianity is a "first-person plural" religion, where communal worship, service, fellowship, and learning are indispensable for grounding and forming individual faith. The strength of Christianity in North America depends on the presence of healthy, spiritually nourishing, well-functioning congregations. Congregations are the cradle of Christian faith, the communities in which children of all ages are supported, encouraged, and formed for lives of service. Congregations are the habitat in which the practices of the Christian life can flourish.

As living organisms, congregations are by definition in a constant state of change. Whether the changes are in membership, pastoral leadership, lay leadership, the needs of the community, or the broader culture, a crucial mark of healthy congregations is their ability to deal creatively and positively with change. The fast pace of change in contemporary culture, with its bias toward, not against, change only makes the challenge of negotiating change all the more pressing for congregations.

Vital Worship

At the center of many discussions about change in churches today is the topic of worship. This is not surprising, for worship is at the center of congregational life. To "go to church" means, for most members of congregations, "to go to worship." In *How Do We Worship?*, Mark Chaves begins his analysis with the simple assertion, "Worship is the most central and public activity engaged in by American religious congregations" (Alban Institute, 1999, p. 1). Worship styles are one of the most significant reasons that people choose to join a given congregation. Correspondingly, they are central to the identity of most congregations.

Worship is also central on a much deeper level. Worship is the locus of what several Christian traditions identify as the nourishing center of congregational life: preaching, common prayer, and the celebration of ordinances or sacraments. Significantly, what many traditions elevate to the status of "the means of grace" or even the "marks of the church" are essentially liturgical actions. Worship is central, most significantly, for theological reasons. Worship both reflects and shapes a community's faith. It expresses a congregation's view of God and enacts a congregation's relationship with God and each other.

We can identify several specific factors that contribute to spiritually vital worship and thereby strengthen congregational life.

- Congregations, and the leaders that serve them, need a shared vision for worship that is grounded in more than personal aesthetic tastes. This vision must draw on the deep theological resources of Scripture, the Christian tradition, and the unique history of the congregation.
- Congregational worship should be integrated with the whole life of the congregation. It can serve as the "source and summit" from which all the practices of the Christian life flow. Worship both reflects and shapes the life of the church in education, pastoral care, community service, fellowship, justice, hospitality, and every other aspect of church life.
- The best worship practices feature not only good worship "content," such as discerning sermons, honest prayers, creative artistic contributions, celebrative and meaningful rituals for baptism and the Lord's Supper. They also arise of out of good process, involving meaningful contributions

from participants, thoughtful leadership, honest evalua-
tion, and healthy communication among leaders.

Vital Worship, Healthy Congregations Series

The Vital Worship, Healthy Congregations Series is designed to
reflect the kind of vibrant, creative energy and patient reflection
that will promote worship that is both relevant and profound. It
is designed to invite congregations to rediscover a common vision
for worship, to sense how worship is related to all aspects of congregational life, and to imagine better ways of preparing both better "content" and better "process" related to the worship life of
their own congregations.

It is important to note that strengthening congregational life
through worship renewal is a delicate and challenging task precisely because of the uniqueness of each congregation. This book
series is not designed to represent a single denomination, Christian
tradition, or type of congregation. Nor is it designed to serve as ar-
biter of theological disputes about worship. Books in the series will
note the significance of theological claims about worship, but they
may, in fact, represent quite different theological visions from each
other, or from our work at the Calvin Institute of Christian Worship. That is, the series is designed to call attention to instructive
examples of congregational life and to explore these examples in
ways that allow readers in very different communities to compare
and contrast these examples with their own practice. The models
described in any given book may for some readers be instructive
as examples to follow. For others, a given example may remind
them of something they are already doing well, or something they
will choose not to follow because of theological commitments or
community history.

In *Preaching Ethically: Being True to the Gospel, the Congregation and Yourself*, Ronald Sisk recovers one of the central
dimensions of classical rhetoric that is increasingly important for
postmodern audiences. Personal integrity is—wonderfully—one of
the most important criteria that younger, postmodern congregations are demanding in congregational leadership. They have had

enough of a culture of spin. But while it is hard to be against personal integrity, it is also often very challenging to practice it in the context of ambiguous or personally demanding circumstances. The preacher's own personal difficulties, vexing political realities, and the challenge of working in an information-saturated, but wisdom-deprived culture all make the ethics of preaching more challenging than it first appears. Sisk leads us through some of these challenges with the nuance and empathy only a seasoned pastor can provide.

By promoting encounters with instructive examples from various parts of the body of Christ, we pray that these volumes will help leaders make good judgments about worship in their congregations and that, by the power of God's Spirit, these congregations will flourish.

John D. Witvliet
Calvin Institute for Christian Worship

Preface

Preaching isn't easy. Preaching ethically in twenty-first-century society is especially complex. Examples of unethical preaching abound, with the news media full of the rants and the antics of high-profile preachers. We see preachers pretending to be experts on everything from constitutional history to global warming. In this day of the ubiquitous Internet and its easy downloads, plagiarism in preaching has become a major issue. The comics and the pundits jeer gleefully at preachers who say one thing and do another. Dedicated pastors often don't know whether they are supposed to be chaplains, prophets, politicians, or crusaders. The truth is pastors may need to be a little of all those things, and a good bit more. But how do you preach so as to meet the legitimate needs of your congregation and live up to standards of professionalism and personal integrity?

The great nineteenth-century preacher Phillips Brooks's classic observation that preaching is "truth through personality" reminds us that the gospel we preachers hope to portray always passes through the prism of the preacher's personal expression on its way to the congregation's ears. That prism is colored by our background, education, biases, mood, political leanings, and a host of other factors. Our task is not to attempt to excise all those factors from our preaching. We couldn't anyway. They are often what makes a sermon interesting!

To be true to ourselves and our calling, however, we must take account of how all the various factors that can influence our preaching come into play. And the calling to preach the gospel compels us to attempt to preach in ways that keep the gospel foremost, that treat the congregation fairly, and that are true to our own convictions and our personal integrity.

This book offers guidelines for how to preach ethically in the light of a range of factors that might tempt a preacher to misuse the pulpit. How do you preach about controversial issues? What do you say from the pulpit when your marriage is in trouble? What are the ethics of preaching in times of local or national crisis? How do you write a sermon when you know very little about a subject? Why and how do you feed a congregation a balanced sermonic diet?

From my own twenty years as a pastor, my training in Christian ethics, my attempts as a seminary professor to help fledgling pastors grow, and a lifetime of listening to sermons preached ethically and otherwise, I offer this meditation. If you preach, hope to preach, or listen to preachers, this book is dedicated to you. My hope is that the next generation of preachers will be good stewards of the great privilege of preaching the gospel!

We Should No Longer Be Children

Preaching Your Perspective

The Anton Ministerial Study Group members were proud of what they had achieved. The six of them had developed a lectionary study group that actually included every full-time pastor in town. Baptist, Catholic, Lutheran, Mennonite, Methodist, and Presbyterian, they met once a week in the basement of Resurrection Lutheran to go over scriptures from the Revised Common Lectionary (now *that* had been an interesting compromise!) and to discuss preaching themes for the coming Sunday. Along the way they had learned both to like each other and to appreciate the different perspectives they brought. Most weeks they discovered they were more alike than different.

Today, though, promised to strain their hard-won camaraderie. The readings were those for the third Sunday in Lent, Year B. The Old Testament lesson was the Ten Commandments. And the conversation was veering toward "Thou shalt not kill."

Father Joe spoke first. "This one, at least, we can be clear about," he began. "The Holy Father says the Catholic Church must oppose abortion and capital punishment with every fiber of our being."

John from Anton Baptist jumped in, "I'm sure with you on abortion, Joe! Scripture prohibits that. But we Baptists tend to believe 'An eye for an eye and a tooth for a tooth.' Murderers deserve what they get."

Evelyn, the Presbyterian and the only one in the room with a PhD, demurred. "I'm not at all sure the Scripture is clear on abortion. The Hebrews didn't believe the baby was fully human till it drew its first breath. This text is about committing murder within the covenant community, isn't it?"

Lars, the Mennonite, couldn't contain himself any further. "Wait," he said. "The text says what it says. 'Thou shalt not kill.' That's why we Mennonites have been conscientious objectors all these years. Christians can't kill anybody, preborn or postborn. Nor can Christians serve in the military."

"Sure we can," John shot back. "I was in the army for four years before I went to seminary. Defending our country is one of the most Christian things I've ever done."

"I think that depends on which war you were in," Joe said. "Some wars are just. Some aren't. This recent adventurism doesn't fit any of the criteria for a just war!"

While John was turning red and sputtering, Mary, the Methodist, took the opportunity to jump in. "I think I see what's happening here," she said. "This is one of those texts we all approach from the perspective of our own tradition. The United Methodists officially opposed the invasion of Iraq, so that's the way I'm required to preach." Mary didn't want to mention that as a very young woman she herself had undergone an abortion. In her heart, though, she wondered whether men should have a voice in that debate at all.

"I couldn't live under that kind of authority," John, the Baptist, finally managed to stammer. "I have to do what the Lord and the Scripture tell me to do. Oh, and the deacons, of course. Sometimes I feel like the six of us don't even follow the same Bible!"

"Lutherans approach these kinds of issues as a group," Nate Hanson said, showing his discomfort with confrontation by running his hand through his blond hair. "I don't have to agree with what the synod decides, but I do feel obliged to take their advice seriously." Nate had a feeling he came closest to agreeing with Evelyn, but he really didn't want to get into this. Silence fell. For the first time the group realized how different their approaches were.

We will leave the Anton Ministerial Study Group members to work out their own relationships. Clearly, though, Mary the Methodist had an excellent point. Preaching is shaped by the preacher's perspective. Ethically, one of a preacher's primary obligations has to be to understand and acknowledge her own point of view and the way in which that point of view shapes what she says from the pulpit.

Take, for example, my own communion, the Baptists. Part of the cultural lore of Baptists from their earliest beginnings has been the notion that Baptists are "people of the Book." Ask a Baptist pastor about the content of his preaching, and he will virtually always begin with a statement like "I preach the Bible." Baptists, however, are a culturally and theologically fragmented people. There are some two hundred Baptist groups in the United States, ranging from extremely conservative to quite liberal. There are Baptist Calvinists, Baptist Barthians, Baptist liberationists, and Baptist feminists. There are African American Baptists, Swedish American Baptists, German American Baptists, Chinese American Baptists and Hispanic Baptists, to name a few. There are Baptist groups that divided over slavery and Baptist groups that divided over missions and Baptist groups that divided over baptism itself. Anyone who thinks the Baptist Jerry Falwell and the Baptist Martin Luther King Jr. would preach the same way and with the same emphases simply hasn't been paying attention.

A significant starting place for preaching ethically, therefore, involves developing a clear sense of one's own experiential, theological, contextual, and philosophical perspectives. It is in the interaction of these perspectives within the mind and spirit of the preacher that specific sermons are formed. Sometimes these perspectives will be in conflict. On a given subject, one may find that his theology and his experience, or her personal philosophical convictions and the traditions of her denomination, are in conflict.

When this happens a preacher has to sort through and either rec-oncile these differing perspectives or decide which will take pre-cedence. Growing up white and Baptist in the deep South in the 1950s and 1960s, I was raised to believe that whites and African Americans should live and worship separately. The preachers of my childhood said so from the pulpit. At the same time, the larger American culture was moving decisively in the direction of inte-gration. As a young Christian on the way to becoming a pastor, I had to decide for myself whether to accede to the traditions of my culture and the churches in which I was raised or follow my own reading of Scripture and the teachings of the larger church.

Let's be clear. The core of the gospel itself does not change. All true preaching proclaims the one gospel that is the same yesterday, today, and tomorrow. What does change is how that one gospel is interpreted ethically in different contexts.

Every preacher must walk a similar path of discernment again and again. The remainder of this chapter examines these critical elements that inform one's ethical perspective.

Experience

Your preaching begins with your own experience. Wesleyan teach-ing makes experience one of the four sources of authority in the Christian life, along with tradition, Scripture, and reason. *Experi-ence*, in this sense, is usually interpreted to mean the manner in which the individual's relationship with Christ and the history of that relationship as it is played out in the person's own life col-ors his or her view of reality. If Mary from our ministerial group chooses to preach on the subject of abortion, she cannot do so without taking into account in some fashion her own experience of that procedure and the way she has subsequently worked through that experience within the context of her faith.

In my earlier book *The Competent Pastor*, I talked about the way in which our experience of our family of origin necessarily shapes our subsequent reactions.[1] A preacher who grew up in a close-knit, conservative Christian family on a farm in Minnesota will view life very differently from a preacher who grew up in six different foster homes in a Los Angeles suburb. A male preacher who grew up on that farm in Minnesota may view life very differently from his younger sister, also a preacher, who grew up in precisely the same household. If their tradition did not support women in ministry, her sense of struggling against her upbringing will become a filter through which she views the meaning of the gospel. Her brother, on the other hand, may approach his ministry from the sense of cultural entitlement that many men quite unconsciously bring to pastoral work. He may have a much more difficult time than she does being sensitive to the struggles of the oppressed. Their colleague from Los Angeles may struggle all his life with feelings of abandonment and insecurity that find their way into both the content and the tone of his preaching. Family issues, health issues, race, gender, sexual orientation, denominational crises—all of these and many other facets of our experience come into play.

Hans-Georg Gadamer, a renowned German philosopher who died in 2002 and whose work has been foundational for much of modern hermeneutics, argued that biblical interpretation is limited by the particular historical horizon of the interpreter. Meaning is thus affected both by the horizon of the biblical authors themselves and by the horizons of contemporary interpreters.[2] Even the most educated and sophisticated of us are creatures of our own era and experiences.

This experiential limitation of our perspective in preaching isn't necessarily bad. The church needs people such as Dietrich Bonhoeffer and Martin Luther King Jr. whose very strength derived from the particularity of their experience. It is, rather, a fact of which we who preach must be aware. Our experience and its limitations should lead us to a certain humility of approach, as we acknowledge that other preachers from other times and places may experience and interpret a particular scripture very differently than we do. One can only imagine, for example, the difference in interpretations of Paul's letter to Philemon by a second-century slave owner and a twenty-first-century African American. Indeed, one could hardly imagine them interpreting that letter with any significant similarities.

Theology

A second significant factor in any preacher's homiletical approach has to be his or her theological perspective. Every preacher views Scripture and life in general through a theologically conditioned interpretive lens. For most of us, that lens is the theological tradition in which we have been raised or trained. Like fish in water or birds in the air, we may not even realize how our surroundings affect us. I experienced one rather dramatic example of this truth as a Baptist teenager, long before I ever dreamed of preaching. One Sunday evening I visited a Methodist friend's youth group. When the Methodist preacher, who was leading the group that evening, found out that I was Baptist, he engaged me in discussion about whether immersion or sprinkling was the proper mode for baptism. He took great delight in citing Jesus's question about John the Baptist, "What did you go out into the wilderness to look at? A reed shaken by the wind?" (Matt. 11:7). His argument was that John used a reed to splash water on those he was baptizing. The preacher took this as biblical support for sprinkling. I knew that as a Baptist I wasn't supposed to agree, but I had no idea why.

The forty years since that uncomfortable Sunday evening have taught me a great deal about biblical interpretation, but they have done nothing to change my realization that night that a person's theology necessarily colors that person's perspective. Pentecostals argue that the rest of the church sadly neglects preaching about the Holy Spirit, and Calvinists turn themselves inside out working to prove that God is both fully sovereign and fully good. Feminist theologians look for the explicit or implied role of women in biblical interactions, and postmodernists spend a great deal of energy searching for the other, the oppressed, as the proper subject of preaching.[3]

Again, as with experience, preaching honestly from one's own theological perspective is not wrong. Indeed, to do so is far better than preaching from a confusion of varying viewpoints or even from no clear perspective at all. What is necessary ethically is for the preacher to be aware of the interpretive theological lens being used and to communicate that awareness to the congregation.

The opening vignette left the impression that some members of the Anton ministerial group may have lacked an understanding of the way in which their own theological tradition colored their interpretations of Scripture. No preacher in the twenty-first century can afford such naïveté. We live in a world where so many forces vie for people's loyalties that we cannot hope to compete unless we can say both where we stand and why.

Am I suggesting that preachers should not hold decided theological opinions? Absolutely not. The danger with such lack of awareness is rather that the preacher will assume that his own tradition possesses the truth to the exclusion of others. That assumption leads to a kind of theological absolutism that cuts off the dialogue necessary for meaningful witness in a pluralistic world. Lack of awareness of our place in the theological spectrum makes us myopic, as we fail to perceive that others may have a valid point of view. It may also impoverish our preaching, as we concentrate on one favorite portion of the gospel message. If the only image I use for God is Father, what do I have to say to the person whose earthly father was cold or distant or abusive? If I preach only about dramatic conversions, how does my preaching help those (by far the majority) whose commitment to Christ has grown gradually across the years?

Tradition

Every preacher operates within the context of a tradition. Elements of that tradition are formalized in terms of the covenants pastors make with their denomination at ordination and with their congregation at installation. For many church folk and pastors, though, the tradition is more culturally enforced—for example, "Lutherans don't do it that way." Some traditions are more rigid than others. In any tradition, though, there are some things you can say in your church and some things you can't.

If the church is independent of any denominational affiliation, those boundaries are the boundaries of the congregation's own statement of faith. For most of us, though, the boundaries that govern our homiletical endeavors are the covenantal and traditional boundaries of the denomination within which we are ordained and serve. Father Joe in our opening vignette is duty-bound to preach a certain way regarding the issue of abortion. If he didn't preach within particular boundaries, he would violate the Roman Catholic Church's teaching on the subject, on pain of losing his pulpit. Similarly, Evelyn the Presbyterian will be informed by her own church's much more prochoice stance on the subject. A presbytery will be less likely to enforce uniformity in social teaching than a Roman Catholic diocese. Many mainline Protestant groups discipline pastors only in extreme cases. Still, if she wishes to remain faithful to Presbyterian teaching, Evelyn will caution against taking abortion lightly, but she will also uphold the conscience of the individual woman as the place where the decision is made.

Baptist polity is much more confusing. John's denomination may have a statement on the issue, but he will be accountable to preach in accordance with that statement only if his parishioners (a) know what the statement is and (b) strongly agree that it defines their own understanding of Baptist faith. Many people these days would assume that Baptists would be antiabortion, but I personally served one church that was fairly aggressively prochoice and two others that would have been profoundly uncomfortable had I brought the issue into the pulpit at all.

Most of us preach within a particular tradition because that is where we were raised or converted. Some of us choose a tradition because we find ourselves in substantial agreement with its theological understanding of the essentials of the faith (God, Christ, salvation, and so forth) and its social teachings (personal morality, war and peace, the role of women in the church, and so forth). Some may choose a tradition because of its ecclesiology. I have seen some seminary students become United Methodists because of the tradition of itineracy and others leave the Methodists for precisely the same reason. Any of us may have points at which we disagree with the dominant strain of teaching within our own communion. The thoughtful preacher will maintain an ongoing dialogue with her tradition, seeking to understand how her preaching should both be informed by and contribute to the tradition within which she serves.

The United Methodist Council of Bishops, for example, has formally opposed the war in Iraq. For Mary the Methodist, the homiletical considerations might include, among other things, the occupations of her parishioners, the sentiment of her parish council, whether her church is located near a military base, and the degree to which her bishop or district superintendent has advised preaching on the issue. These considerations may or may not be determinative for her on a given Sunday. Still, a wise preacher will both be aware of such homiletical minefields and negotiate them carefully.

Ethics

One might ask, of course, whether we really need to discuss ethics as a separate category for homiletical formation. Don't our experience, theology, and tradition work together to create our homiletical ethics? They do, but a preacher's ethical perspective is more than the sum of its parts. I would argue that a conversation goes on in the preacher's life between his own ethical perspective and his understanding of what is important in the pulpit. Duke Divinity School ethicist Stanley Hauerwas talks about ethics as character, one's dominant approach to the challenges of life. My own ethics teacher Glen Stassen argues that in many ways, people's ethical perspectives are profoundly affected by what he calls their "first adult experience." For the generation that came of age in the 1940s, World War II, with its social unity, its intense patriotism, and its appreciation for the American way of life provided the background for that first adult experience. When the children of that generation grew up during the Vietnam era, the cynicism and distrust of authority those children felt was virtually incomprehensible to their parents. In each case, the experience resulted in a perspective on life that tended to affect decision making far beyond the initial experience itself.

Such a perspective may be predominantly religious, but it may not be. It could be sociopolitical, as in the examples above. It could be gender-political, as in those people whose homiletics is formed largely by their personal view of the role of women in American life or of the place of gays in the church and society. It could be ethnically driven. Some African American preachers focus on the meaning of the gospel for the struggles of black people in American society. Some preach from the perspective that "You cannot be a Christian and a Democrat." Having spent time myself on both coasts, in the north, in the south, and along the Mason-Dixon Line, I learned long ago that for many people, their view of the faith is determined by their regional perspectives and loyalties. Otherwise well-informed and highly educated people may be quite provincial in their perceptions of life. Liberationists, womanists, postmodernists, liberals, conservatives, and wishy-washies all have an ethical perspective that affects their homiletical approach.

Perspective and Preaching

My point is simple. Every preacher approaches the preaching task with some sort of worldview. Because even those of us who claim we "just preach the Bible" come to the preparation of sermons with an inevitable bias, we cannot preach ethically unless we both seek to become aware of our own biases and to make those biases known in appropriate ways to our listeners. These, then, are two questions the preacher must ask herself: (1) What are the experiences, theological perspectives, group loyalties, and personal ethical values that affect my own homiletical approach? And (2) how do I practice appropriate self-disclosure as I preach from week to week? The answer to the first of these questions may take a lifetime to unravel. The answer to the second goes back to one of the most basic principles of modern homiletics.

Writing in the late nineteenth century, the American preacher Phillips Brooks defined preaching as "truth through personality." By that, of course, he meant in part that the person of the preacher inevitably colors what he or she says from the pulpit. In some ways both the questions I have posed above are implied in Brooks's assertion. How do we recognize the way in which our own unique perspective colors what we say, and how do we communicate that awareness authentically (truthfully) to our hearers?

Homiletician Thomas Long, in his influential introductory text, *The Witness of Preaching,* identifies witness as a controlling image for the work of the preacher.[4] By that he means that ultimately what the preacher has to offer is what he or she has experienced. In a subsequent book he talks about the importance of the old Protestant concept of testimony. Long underscores the importance of these personal stories of the faith. We describe what has happened to us.

In my own preaching, *I* am speaking, in my case, as a fifty-seven-year-old, white, southern male from a working-class Democratic-party background; raised during the Vietnam era; formed by the Baptist perspective on the faith; educated in Arkansas, New York, and Kentucky; working in a northern, evangelical, and ecumenical theological seminary. The more transparent I am about who I am, the more my listeners can gauge for themselves the degree to which my biases may affect what I say.

In addition, to a great degree all I can say is what has happened to *me.* As Haddon Robinson, a longtime Gordon-Conwell professor and preacher with an evangelical perspective, says in his definition of expository preaching, biblical preaching happens "through a historical, grammatical, and literary study of a passage in its context, *which the Holy Spirit first applies to the personality and experience of the preacher,* then through the preacher, applies to the hearers"[5] (emphasis added).

As the preachers from the Anton Ministerial Study Group demonstrate, this transparency in preaching requires ongoing personal effort both to know yourself well and to remain objective about how who you are informs your preaching. One might say that the conversation is between distance and intimacy. You must remain intimately aware of the influences that shape you and at the same time be able to evaluate those influences honestly. You must know yourself well enough to be able to testify how you have responded to those formative influences. An ethical preacher first honestly and unashamedly preaches her own perspective.

CHAPTER 2

Simple Statement of the Truth

Preaching Your Own Work

Sunday morning at 8:05, Pastor Ellen Freeman walked into her study and sat down heavily behind her desk. The truth was, she felt slightly sick to her stomach. She hadn't meant it to happen, but in twenty-five minutes, for the first time in her career, she was going to preach someone else's sermon instead of her own.

Like most pastors, Ellen had experienced dry periods from time to time. Sometimes her schedule just got too busy or the words simply wouldn't flow. Usually she managed to cobble something together, even if it was less than stellar. Often she had adapted someone else's outline or used someone else's key illustration. Still, in ten years as a pastor, she had never yet done what she was about to do—walk into St. Luke's pulpit with a sermon she had had no part in writing.

On Friday it had seemed to make a lot of sense. With two funerals behind her that week and most of Saturday committed for a big wedding, Ellen had realized her planned sermon on forgiveness was just not going to gel. In desperation she had gone to the Internet looking for sources. Suddenly there it was—a complete, elegant sermon on just the text she had chosen. It had been written by a respected but not really famous female preacher in another state. Reading it, Ellen was convinced there was no way she would do any better. "Surely," she thought, "the congregation would be better off hearing this than anything I'll be able to compose." Just then the phone had rung with news of another crisis. A member was being taken to the emergency room with a possible heart attack. So Ellen had swallowed the lump in her throat, printed out the sermon, and headed out to the hospital.

But now she wasn't so sure. Wasn't this crossing a line? What would the elders say if they knew? What would her husband say? Should she just tell the congregation what had happened? She looked at the clock. It was 8:23. She got up and headed for the sanctuary.

An Act of Integrity

On the surface, the premise of this chapter seems almost absurdly simple. Preaching must be an act of integrity. You do your own work. This is not only the right thing to do, but it is also what the church universally expects of its preachers. You don't borrow other people's work or present someone else's words or experiences as your own. Plagiarism in the church of Jesus is a theological contradiction in terms. We are to be people committed to the truth.

And yet I have known a number of preachers over the years who have lied with their preaching—stood in the pulpit "before God and everybody" and pretended someone else's work was their own. Occurring often enough to be embarrassing for the American church as a whole, some of those incidents have become scandalously public.

So what is going on here? Why does a seemingly simple principle of preaching, "Do your own work," prove to be so difficult in practice for many otherwise exemplary Christian leaders? The answers might well be as varied as the individuals themselves. Ellen, in our opening vignette, would probably see herself as a victim of circumstance. I do believe it might be useful, however, to look at some factors that may encourage or at least permit this kind of moral failure.

Anonymity

A number of years ago I taught a class on New Testament ethics for a local university. One of the students in that class, an ordained minister, turned in a book review that didn't seem to match the writing style of his other work. Suspicious, I logged onto Amazon. com and began to read the reviews of the book posted there. In less than five minutes, I had him. Substantial pieces of his paper had been lifted verbatim from that Web site.

When I confronted the student, I asked him why he had attempted such a thing. I got a two-part answer that I found very telling. "First," he said, "I didn't think anyone would ever notice." The anonymity of the Web had made him think it unlikely I would discover what he had done. The information was there. It was easy to obtain and claim as his own. And the false privacy he thought he had at home working in his study allowed him to ignore the reality that the Internet is a very public medium.

As I have pondered that incident over the years, I have come to believe that this false perception of anonymity plays a significant role in enabling plagiarism in contemporary preaching. The Internet plays the role of the chief tempter. With so much sermonizing out there, accessing those sermons is absurdly easy. My own favorite Christian ethics Web site posts a half-dozen or more new sermons every week. Hundreds of churches post their pastors' sermons. Homiletics journals post sermons. Historians and theologians post sermons they discover in their research. Anyone who seeks a sermon on virtually any scriptural text or topic can find plenty of help through Internet search engines in less than half an hour.

Connect that profusion of material with the fact that the number of potential biblical texts is finite, though the number of combinations of texts is not, and you produce a situation ripe for temptation. "Why do it myself?" the preacher reasons. "Chances are someone else has already done it better than I ever could." Stir in situational factors such as Ellen's workload that week, and the pressure to plagiarize proliferates. All you have to do is be a little more clever than my student was, and you can probably get away with it.

Contempt

Second, though he took a while to say it, my student finally admitted that he saw himself as much more theologically conservative than I was and therefore as on a different moral plane. Because he thought I was more liberal (from his perspective, inferior), he thought he was somehow justified in deceiving me. In short, the second element in his reasoning was contempt for the audience. He didn't think he owed me the truth. I wasn't as spiritual as he was.

Notice that Ellen in the opening scenario is focused on her own problem. She hasn't had enough time to do work that would meet her personal standard of performance. But instead of simply being honest with the congregation, she views the sermon as a polished package she must somehow deliver. Rather than seeing herself as a fellow pilgrim with the congregation on the way of faith, she has excluded them from the world in which she lives and struggles. She assumes that they somehow cannot understand the reality of a week in which one might not be able to get everything done. In effect, she puts herself above them.

One can easily see how such contempt might be aggravated by a host of other factors. The preacher who sees herself as serving a less educated congregation than she really deserves, the preacher who views the governing board as too harsh, or the preacher grown cynical from too much exposure to human failure and too anemic a theology of grace might be vulnerable to developing contempt for her listeners. Contempt then poisons the well of motivation to share oneself honestly with a congregation.

Pressure

When I remember that student who plagiarized his book review, I find it somewhat easier to forgive him if I consider the pressure he must have been under. Ellen would probably argue that pressure was the determinative factor for her. She really did have a lot to do that week. She really did not feel she had adequate time to prepare. She really did want to do well for her congregation. Performance pressure and time pressure worked together to produce what she saw as an impossible situation.

Part of the performance pressure here is the dark side of an essentially good trend, the professionalization of ministry in the past century. Preaching is one of the competencies that people expect of their pastors and most pastors expect of themselves. What has happened, though, is that congregations and pastors increasingly view the sermon as a discrete entity, in effect entertainment that, like a half-hour television program, must be cut and polished both to delight the audience and to fit seamlessly into its allotted time in the worship service.

The more a worship service is viewed this way, as a package of entertainment, the more distance is created between the preacher and the audience. Notice the change of terms. *Congregation* becomes *audience*. A preacher whose dominant concern is that he or she deliver an acceptable package has lost that essential personal connection with the congregation that transforms a speech into a pastoral encounter. He or she has moved away from intimate Christian fellowship and toward compartmentalization of life. Like Elmer Gantry in the classic novel of the same name, the preacher becomes capable of saying one thing in the pulpit and doing quite another outside it.

In a given week, time pressure may seriously aggravate matters. Many preachers view the act of preaching as perhaps the most important thing they do all week. They very much want to do it well. Ellen believed she simply did not have time to prepare well on her own. Going down the road she took, though, preachers quickly lose touch with both biblical and theological reality.

Biblically, the apostle Paul, no mean preacher, nonetheless assures the Corinthians, "I did not come proclaiming the mystery of God to you in lofty words or wisdom. For I decided to know nothing among you except Jesus Christ, and him crucified. And I came to you in weakness and in fear and in much trembling. My speech and my proclamation were not with plausible words of wisdom . . ." (1 Cor. 2:1-4). It wasn't eloquence Paul had to share with the Corinthians. It was his experience and his faith.

Theologically, Karl Barth's lectures on homiletics put a positive slant on this idea of Paul's that we preachers bring to our preaching who we really are in this given moment, our experience and our faith. In his lecture on originality, Barth observes:

> It is as the persons they are that preachers are called to this task, as these specific people with their own characteristics and histories. It is as the persons they are that they have been selected and called. This is what is meant by originality. Pastors are not to adopt a role. . . . They are not to be Luthers, churchmen, prophets, visionaries, or the like. They are simply to be themselves and to expound the text as such. Preaching is the responsible word of a person of our own time. Having heard myself, I am called upon to pass on what I have heard. Even as ministers, it matters that these persons be what they are.[1]

How, then, might Ellen have dealt authentically with the pressure she felt that Sunday after that awful week? The first step would have been to be honest with herself about her motivation. By focusing on performance at the expense of integrity, she cared more about looking good than she cared about being honest with the congregation. After repenting of that particular sin, the second step would be to search for some honest way to preach that morning, even though she could not perform up to her own personal standards.

The straightforward approach is best. As she enters the pulpit to preach she could say something like, "Unfortunately the demands of being pastor this week left me without time to prepare adequately for this morning's worship. So I'm going to do something unusual. I'm going to preach a sermon prepared by someone else. On today's subject, I've discovered that [Name] says well what I would like to say. So, listen with me as we all hear these fine words together, and may the Lord bless them to our hearts." With this statement, Ellen has acknowledged her failure to prepare, she has made it clear that this is an anomaly, she has given credit to the person who prepared the words, and she has reminded the congregation that it is ultimately the Spirit to whom worshipers listen. She has also implicitly promised that using someone else's work is not the norm.

Could she get into trouble for adopting such a course of action? Certainly she could. But she will get into far less trouble for openly acknowledging what she is doing than she would if it became known that she had preached someone else's work and *not* acknowledged that fact.

Long term, of course, experiencing frequent occasions when one lacks the time to prepare a sermon needs to be seen as an indication of serious problems in one's work patterns. In twenty years as a pastor, that simply never happened to me. Was I more industrious or more virtuous than others? I don't think so. It is more a matter of priorities. As a preaching pastor, I saw the preparation of the sermon as *the* primary duty of the week. Everything else I did had to find its place within the reality of that commitment. Honestly, I believe God helped me do that. No matter what was happening in a given week, if I gave each day to God, the time I needed seemed to be there. So am I contradicting myself? Did Ellen have enough time to prepare a sermon or didn't she? I believe she did. The problem here is that she let other considerations keep her from doing the best job she could that week, given the time she had.

This is not to say that there might not be legitimate reasons why one would find it difficult to preach in a given week. Illness, a family crisis, and many other unexpected events do arise. Tom Long points us particularly toward the preacher's experience of a personal spiritual or creative dry spell. "These times," he says, "should neither surprise nor dismay us. In some ways the best counsel is to acknowledge that all preachers have them, to expect them, and to allow them to run their course."[2] In the providence of God, our own neediness may even in some ways serve the spiritual growth of those to whom we preach. The congregation needs to know that we are as human as they are. Otherwise they view us as living by some spiritual standard they could never attain.

The Question of Sources

So when is it ethical for a preacher to use someone else's work as a source? Can you quote a sentence? A paragraph? More? Do you always have to cite the source verbally, even if it is homiletically

awkward to do so? What if you find a terrific outline online and
develop that outline yourself? Do you then have to tell the church
that the structure of your sermon comes from John Claypool or
Haddon Robinson or Norman Vincent Peale?

First, remember that preaching is not usually about telling
church people something they have never heard before, certainly
not doctrinally. Indeed, that way lies heresy. Rather, preaching is
about proclaiming eternal truths in fresh terms so that contemporary audiences may hear the ancient faith for themselves and apply
it to contemporary life. A wide variety of interpretive aids, from
commentaries to sermons to collections of illustrations, are both
helpful and necessary. The preacher needs a good library, a good
record-keeping process, and a good filing system. No one is either
sufficiently scholarly or sufficiently creative to preach without that
kind of input and assistance.

Second, therefore, using quotations, images, stories, and even
outlines from other preachers and writers is a legitimate part of
the preparation task. No preacher needs to be placed under the
burden of creating every sermon from scratch. The issue is not that
of creation but rather of attribution.

Does attribution really matter in a world where there seem to
be precious few genuinely new ideas? I believe it does. All of us
stand on the shoulders of those who have gone before. Acknowledging that debt and making it explicit nourishes our roots in the
history and tradition that have shaped us. Sometimes, to give one
very homely example, I find myself speaking clichés or expressing
attitudes that come down to me from my father. Dad was a good,
honest man, a craftsman who worked with his hands most of his
life. His understanding of the world was limited by his education,
his lack of religious training, and the family system that nurtured
him. But he also displayed an essential kindness and a kind of
earthy wisdom, especially in practical matters. When I quote my
dad, I pay homage to his considerable influence in shaping my life.
I acknowledge that my own opinions, like those of everyone who
hears me, are a composite derived from many sources.

Such attribution helps protect preachers from the intellectual
arrogance that assumes we owe no debt. It thus cultivates humility within the preacher and connects us and our hearers to those

who have gone before. Sometimes, especially as we grow older, we find that we have heard an idea so many times or that we have used it so often ourselves that we no longer remember precisely when, how, or from whom it came to us. In these cases, the very act of searching for a source may help reconnect us with our intellectual and spiritual roots. It is important not to be legalistic about this. But whether we are successful in locating a source or not, the search confirms us in the spiritual discipline of humility.

What is essential for the preacher's integrity is that she never give people the impression that she has created work that is not in fact her own. This does not mean that a sermon need be filled with dozens of awkward citations of sources. It does mean that a preacher should learn to give credit as part of the flow of his work. I have said things such as, "John Claypool's interpretation of this passage tells me . . ." The sentence takes only a moment, but it both acknowledges the preacher's debt and acknowledges the preacher's own responsibility for what follows. In other words, you need to find a way to say, "It isn't John Claypool preaching here. It's Ron Sisk. But I got this really good idea from him." To fail to acknowledge such a debt is to cross the line from research to plagiarism. Ellen in our opening vignette crosses that line.

Writing in *Review and Expositor* a number of years ago, the Baptist homiletics professor Raymond Bailey wondered why homiletics texts devote so little space to the ethics of preaching.[3] He suggested, "Perhaps this is because they assume the common standards of propriety for academics, politics, business, and literature with regard to respect for the audience, respect for the work of others, and respect for truth will prevail."[4] Unfortunately, if such an assumption ever was valid, that is no longer the case. In the twenty-first century we must say it plainly. Do your own work. Give credit to the work of others. Anything less denies the very calling we espouse.

CHAPTER 3

Let Your *Yes!* Be *Yes!*

Preaching without Manipulation

Sunday morning again. As he lay comfortable in his bed waiting for the alarm, Matt tried to think of a fresh excuse. The problem was that Matt had gotten to the point that he didn't want to go to worship any more. Being sixteen was tough enough without going on a major guilt trip every Sunday morning. And ever since the new pastor had come six months ago, guilt trips at First Church had become an every-Sunday excursion.

Andy O'Bannion, the new pastor at First Church, was a little bantam rooster of a man, about five feet six inches, maybe one-hundred-fifty pounds, but you would never think about his size once he stepped into the pulpit. He shouted. He paced. He sweated. He cried. He told mesmerizing stories of sinners in danger of eternal damnation. Every sermon ended with an altar call. And staid old First Church found itself writhing in an extended agony of self-examination.

It was all so confusing. Like most kids in his denomination, Matt had made the usual commitments at the usual time in the usual way. Till Pastor Andy came, he had felt as secure in his faith as any sixteen-year-old is likely to feel. Sure, he had questions. Sure, he doubted some parts of Christian doctrine. No, he wasn't quite as pure as his parents seemed to think he was. But mostly Matt had liked being a part of the faith his family had followed in that church for more than one hundred years.

Now he just wasn't sure any more. Was Pastor Andy right? If he wasn't, why did Matt feel so bad? Andy seemed to think that if you didn't see things his way, you were in real trouble with God. Matt didn't like that feeling. He wasn't sure he liked Pastor Andy. But he was afraid not to take the pastor seriously. After all, Andy was the pastor, right? And the pastor was supposed to know, wasn't he? What if God really was that angry? Matt groaned and rolled over, pulling the pillow over his head and stuffing it round his ears. Maybe he just wouldn't hear the alarm.

Matt represents a host of folk both within and outside the church who have been subjected to manipulation by preachers down through the years. It isn't tough at all to remember some of the more sensational examples—Jim Jones convincing his Jonestown followers to join him in mass suicide, Oral Roberts telling his TV audience God would kill him unless they sent in a certain amount of money by a given deadline. Many of us who preach have an inherent horror of abusing our position, a horror fueled by our repulsion at extreme instances like those. We have no trouble saying, "By all means, don't do that!"

The real issue, however, is considerably more complicated. Preaching is, after all, an inherently persuasive exercise. Paul told Timothy, "Proclaim the message; be persistent whether the time is favorable or unfavorable; convince, rebuke, and encourage . . ." (2 Tim. 4:2), and preachers are taught to own this urgency as their solemn duty. In 2006 the Christian businessman and preacher Ben J. Katt released a book titled *The Power of Persuasive Preaching*.[1] The book is essentially a fictionalized version of a series of conversations between an experienced sales coach and a pastor. The coach mentors the pastor on how to preach more persuasively. At one point the two protagonists hold a conversation concerning the relationship between persuasion and manipulation. They agree that people tend to perceive persuasion as good and manipulation as bad. The coach, however, argues that *all* persuasive speech is manipulation: "I've noticed people use two definitions [for manipulation]. The first concerns the act of influencing people's thoughts, feelings, and behaviors. The second refers to the intentions behind that influence."[2] It is, he says, "the same animal by different names." In other words, Katt argues that preachers are always attempting to influence people's thoughts, feelings, and behaviors. The question is not *whether* we seek to manipulate people. We do. That, in fact, is what we are called to do. The call of the preacher is to encourage people to connect with the God of Jesus Christ and to change their behavior as a result of that connection. The question is *how* we encourage them. Do we seek to influence our hearers ethically or unethically? In many ways, this is an issue of how we preachers do corporate pastoral care.

While I feel almost as uncomfortable writing Katt's language as you probably feel reading it, I do believe he makes a useful point here. The arbiters of twentieth- and twenty-first-century culture have delighted in highlighting the abuse of the preaching office through Jim Jones–type scandals. One could easily be left with the impression that *any* attempt to influence people, even legitimate encouragement and challenge, is somehow suspect. That is not the case. Preaching by its very nature is intended to persuade the listener in some fashion. Still, though, the question remains as to what manipulation is legitimate. In the rest of this chapter I attempt to set criteria for legitimately persuasive preaching. To do so as clearly as possible, I choose to reject Katt's assertion that *all* persuasive speech is manipulation and draw a distinction between preaching as manipulation and preaching as persuasion.

Truth

The most important criterion for nonmanipulative persuasion is that what the preacher says must, to the best of the preacher's knowledge, be true. While such an assertion seems self-evident, the waters get muddy very quickly indeed. No doubt Pastor Andy believed the preaching that so upset Matt was true. But are we talking about scientific truth, doctrinal truth, emotional truth, relational truth, or some combination of two or more of these ways of understanding reality? Without attempting a philosophy textbook (which I am truthfully not qualified to write anyway!), let's look briefly at each of these four concepts.

Scientific Truth

Scientific truth is defined provisionally and observationally. Observable phenomena suggest hypotheses that are tested and revised in an ongoing process. Scientifically, the preacher's responsibility is to speak about the world as he or she understands it to be. If a preacher understands that the world was not created in six twenty-four-hour days but says from the pulpit that it was, that statement is unacceptable, regardless of why he or she makes it. It represents an attempt to manipulate a congregation's view of reality in an unethical way. By the same token, a preacher who believes the world *was* created in six twenty-four-hour days is obligated to preach that as well. Scientific truth at any particular moment in history is based on current understanding. The truth the preacher is obligated to speak is truth as he or she knows it.

An important corollary of this idea is that the preacher needs to maintain a healthy reluctance to condemn or reject scientific findings, provisional though they may be. A scientific finding that appears to contradict Scripture may not, in fact, do so. Often Scripture and science are talking about different ways of perceiving reality. One operates in the realm of the spirit. The other operates in the realm of observable phenomena. Scripture is not a book of science, nor was it ever intended to be. Modern concepts of scientific investigation and experimentation postdate the biblical era by more than a millennium. Darwin's theory of evolution, for example, is simply a provisional theory about how the development of life on earth progressed. It does not speak to the issue of first causes. The scriptural account of creation, on the other hand, speaks poetically of Who is responsible for the beauty and variety of creation. The two are not incompatible. They are dealing with different perspectives on the story.

In the long term, the restriction of science to observable phenomena is not a problem for thoughtful Christians. We believe, after all, that God is the source of all truth. Every true thing comes from God. Therefore we have no reason to fear any scientific perception or proposition that is demonstrated to be true. Advancing science does not diminish God's authority. Rather, it sheds light on the infinite complexity and variety of God's creation.

The preacher's obligation to preach what is scientifically or objectively true extends to every fact, from the attendance numbers for last week's services to the struggles of her own prayer life. I don't mean we preachers must tell our congregations everything we think and feel. Rather, we have a prima facie obligation to tell the truth as best we know it.

Doctrinal Truth

Provisional though it is, many people in our day tend to think of scientific truth as the only truth. Doctrinal truth, similarly, is a matter of perception. Roman Catholic preachers may believe fervently that infant baptism is a necessary remedy for the consequences of original sin. Baptist preachers may believe just as fervently that infants exist in a state of grace until they reach the age of the capacity for moral choice. Both are obligated to preach the truth as they understand it. In one sense, the entire corpus of systematic theology may be viewed as the record of the church's ongoing search for doctrinal truth.

Perhaps the most helpful thing for preachers to keep in mind regarding doctrine is that even our most deeply held convictions are just that—convictions. They represent what we believe to be true doctrinally. We preachers need to recognize that preaching a particular doctrinal perspective as though all other possible views on the subject were evil may, as with Gamaliel and the Sanhedrin in Acts, place us in the position of opposing the work of God.

Doctrinal understandings change. In 2006, for example, the Evangelical Lutheran Church in America (ELCA) was engaged in conversations with the Mennonites, who trace their roots to sixteenth-century European Anabaptists, and the statements of sixteenth-century Lutherans had become problematic for those conversations. Martin Luther himself is reported to have suggested that all Anabaptists should be immersed, permanently. The ELCA, as a part of those conversations, formally apologized for Luther and Philipp Melanchthon's sixteenth-century condemnation of Anabaptists. This is not to say that one would expect an ELCA preacher to embrace the primacy of believer's baptism, even if he or she happened to believe that was true. Those ordained leaders within a tradition have an obligation to support the teachings of that tradition. This is to say that even doctrinal understandings may evolve and change over time.

Emotional Truth

Emotional truth refers to the emotional condition of preacher and congregation as a sermon is being preached. Is the preacher aware of all the factors that make her feel a particular way about a given subject? Can a pastor going through a divorce preach responsibly when a text about divorce turns up in the Sunday lectionary? What if her husband was unfaithful and the text is about adultery? Is the congregation emotionally capable of hearing what needs to be said? How does a preacher choose when or whether to address emotionally controversial subjects? To what degree can a preacher use emotion to legitimate ends within a sermon? When is the use of emotion in preaching illegitimate?

An excellent example of the complexity of this concept took place in my own state of South Dakota during the contentious 2006 election season. The state was to vote on a law that would have banned almost all abortions in South Dakota. Church folk weighed in passionately on both sides of the issue. Sermons were preached on the subject in a high percentage of the state's pulpits. Every one of those instances involved a preacher with a particular perspective, a denominational viewpoint (in some cases a denominational mandate), and listeners who had thoughts and emotional responses created by specific experience or lack of experience with the issue. Because this was such an emotional issue for so many, people on both sides found themselves out of sync with the positions espoused from the pulpits of their home congregations. Some left their congregations as a result of those sermons. Clearly what was emotionally true for some was emotionally false for others.

Many preachers are adept at producing an emotional response within a congregation. *Pathos* is one of the primary characteristics of Aristotelian rhetoric. It enjoys a long and honored history as a legitimate tactic in public speaking. Appealing to congregation members' emotions is an important persuasive tool in preaching. The question that must be addressed here concerns the boundary between persuasion and manipulation. When does an emotive tale move from legitimate to illegitimate? When does emotional persuasion become emotional manipulation? As a preacher, how can you tell the difference?

Along with pathos, the other two major characteristics of Aristotelian rhetoric are *logos,* understood as the intellectual content of a speech, and *ethos*, understood as the relationship of the audience to the one who speaks.[3] I believe logos and ethos provide important correctives to the use of pathos in a sermon. The preacher's use of emotion is limited by the standard of intellectual honesty. Whenever getting the people to do what the preacher wants becomes more important than telling the people the truth, the preacher has crossed a line. Similarly, whenever the preacher uses his or her status to try to get listeners to do something they would not otherwise do, the preacher has abused that relationship.

Not long ago I saw a trusted preacher tell members that a course of action she wanted them to approve in a congregational vote was God's will. In effect, she left no room for them to think for themselves or to disagree with her opinion. She even misapplied a scripture passage to make her argument. The people who listen to us preachers week by week offer us their trust. They expect that we will follow the highest possible standards of biblical scholarship and personal integrity in what we say. To do any less in the attempt to promote our own agenda is to enter the realm of emotional abuse.

Relational Truth

Emotional truth feeds into the fourth concept I wish to discuss, relational truth. How a preacher feels or thinks about a subject often will not cohere with how her congregation feels or thinks.

Preachers regularly find themselves dealing with the question of whether they can say what they wish to say about a subject and maintain a good relationship with the congregation at the same time.

In the segregated South of my childhood, preachers had to decide whether they would speak from their pulpits for or against civil rights for African Americans—or avoid the issue altogether. For the sake of their relationship with their congregations, many chose the latter path. Some of those who chose to speak for civil rights lost their pulpits. Some experienced real physical danger. I knew one preacher who preached on civil rights and was greeted with a fist to the jaw by the first person out of the sanctuary after the service.

Relational truth comes into play in preaching in other ways as well. One preacher under whom I served had a habit of breaking into tears during his sermons. The congregation was left with the distinct impression that this man lived on the emotional edge. Inherently kind, they gave him great leeway in preaching, even though he frequently said unkind things to and about them during his sermons. His ongoing family troubles, which were many and varied, while not mentioned from the pulpit, became the subtext of his relationship with the congregation. Nobody wanted to confront him with his emotional abuse of the congregation because he himself seemed too fragile. In effect, congregation members served as codependent enablers of the pastor's personal and professional dysfunction.

Homiletics professor Ronald J. Allen writes extensively in his book *Hearing the Sermon* of the way in which the relationship between the preacher and the congregation affects how the congregation hears a sermon.[4] He points out, among other things, the importance of "the congregation's perception that the preacher lives in a way that is consistent with what the preacher says, that the preacher thinks sensitively and meaningfully about life."[5] Clearly this congregational perception of the preacher is as comprehensive and varied as the whole scope of the preacher's interactions with her congregation and community. For example, as a pastor, I made it a point not to be active in partisan politics, though politics is one of my passions. I knew that partisan involvement on my part would make it impossible for some in my congregation to hear what I had to say. Members from another political party might well find it difficult to trust the truth of what I had to say about a whole range of issues. (Later in this book, I deal more fully with the specific issue of what the preacher says about politics from the pulpit.)

The key to relational truth in preaching thus lies largely outside the pulpit itself. I once sat in a Volkswagen Beetle in a church parking lot with my friend Mickey Anders and the late preacher and homiletician John R. Claypool. The three of us were talking about the preacher's ability to speak to a congregation on difficult subjects. Claypool said, "You marry them, you bury the old, you baptize the young, you sit up with them when they're sick or bereaved, and in the process you earn the right to speak and be heard." A congregation to whom a preacher has been true in that way will grant the preacher great freedom in what she says.

The preacher's obligation is to be worthy of that trust. As this book was being written, a prominent Colorado pastor was discovered to have been guilty of a long-term homosexual affair. Aside from the damage to his own family, the greatest sin involved was his betrayal of trust with the congregation he had served for a number of years. Many of the members and participants no doubt found themselves wondering whether they could trust any of what he had said to them from the pulpit all those Sundays.

Intent

Persuasive preaching needs to be true and to intend to be true. Ultimately a preacher's attempts to persuade must give full respect to the listeners' status as independent moral agents, capable of deciding for themselves what they will or will not believe or do. A preacher is in danger of manipulation, on the other hand, whenever he or she regards the listeners as less than equals, as those who must be made to believe or to act in a certain way, whether they choose freely to do so or not. As discussed in chapter 2 with reference to plagiarism, the willingness to manipulate a congregation implies a certain contempt for them, both as individuals and as fellow believers. It suggests that they somehow deserve to be coerced or misled.

When Jesus, on the other hand, says in the Gospel according to John that "true worshipers will worship the Father in spirit and truth" (4:23), the statement implies that those of us who lead the worshiping community have an obligation. We are to shape worship each time, every time, all the time so that it participates authentically in, remains true to, the reality that shapes the cosmos. Anything else belies our calling. Pastor Andy may have had First Church's best interests at heart when he chose to begin his ministry there as he did. But to the extent that he chose manipulative techniques to pursue his ends, he failed to maintain the standard by which a preacher of the gospel must be guided.

CHAPTER 4

I Came to You in Weakness

Preaching and the Pastor's Health

"Ugh . . . Unhh!" Pastor Ron's worst nightmare was coming true. It was Sunday morning. The time for the sermon had come. He stood in front of the congregation and opened his mouth, but no words would come out.

In the moment it took for the congregation to begin to realize something was wrong, he struggled like a drowning man to understand what was happening to him while his life passed in front of his eyes. Was he having a stroke? Was the flu coming back? What in the world was going on?

He had known he was pushing it to preach today. Last week's flu had left him weak and tired. He was no longer contagious. He was back on solid food, but only just. The problem was that today's worship had been carefully planned for weeks. In a rare coincidence for this small church, baptism and communion were planned for both morning services. The people being baptized were folks Ron had worked with personally. Selfishly, he really wanted to be the one to go through that experience with them.

So he had dragged himself to church that morning, gotten through the early service as best he could. By the time he had presided over the baptism during the late service, he had begun to think he had made it. Oddest thing, though—as he was coming out of the baptistry after dressing, he realized his favorite shoes didn't seem to fit this morning. Still, the service was in progress and the congregation was waiting for him. He had to go on.

But now what? Frantic, with his tongue cramping and clinging to the roof of his mouth, Ron motioned to the associate pastor to take over the service and began to hobble painfully off the platform. (His feet were cramping too!) As he did, he saw two doctors from the congregation headed toward the sanctuary door to meet him. Glad as he was to see them, a part of his spirit cringed within him. How embarrassing this all was. How he hated showing weakness in front of the congregation.

That's right, gentle reader. The Pastor Ron in this particular story is me. The flu had left me with an electrolyte imbalance in my system that I aggravated by trying to go back to work too soon. My own determination to go forward, together with my reluctance to acknowledge that I was in trouble, both ruined the morning's worship and resulted in greater embarrassment than calling in sick would have done.[1] I use this minor example of my own foolishness (I have done much worse!) to introduce what for many of us is a major issue. Just how much weakness should a preacher acknowledge in his or her relationship with a congregation? Whether that weakness is physical, spiritual, emotional, or relational—what do we tell, when do we tell it, and how much do we allow our personal struggles to become either the subject or the subtext of our preaching?

Physical Health

Every preacher is first of all a physical human being. We are fat or thin, short or tall, in or out of shape. We grow old. We get sick. Our bodies help make us vulnerable to sin and to stress. The preacher who ignores the reality of this physicality is making a serious mistake. Indeed, some feminist theologians in recent years have focused on embodiment as an interpretive category in understanding our human experience of God.

The apostle Paul appears to be grappling with this issue of how our physical reality affects our preaching in 2 Corinthians when he refers to his "thorn . . . in the flesh" (2 Cor. 12:7). The thorn, he argues, was given him to keep him from being "too elated" by the revelations he had received. The lesson he received from the Lord was "My grace is sufficient for you, for power is made perfect in weakness" (2 Cor. 12:9). Paul was clearly a guy who didn't want to be weak physically. He wanted to be in control. His problem was that his condition, whatever it was, left him obviously not in control in one part of his life. His audiences could see it. Everybody knew. And Paul had to figure out how this obvious weakness could square with the confidence he wanted to express in preaching the gospel.

Unlike Paul, and unlike me that awful Sunday long ago, my own primary physical problem is unseen. As an insulin-dependent diabetic, I must watch my diet, exercise, take injections several times a day, and see my doctor on a regular basis. But no one simply meeting me casually would necessarily know that I am diabetic. While I make it a practice to be very open and matter-of-fact about my diabetes in daily life, I have only rarely mentioned my disease from the pulpit.

That reticence represents an ethical choice for me. On the one hand, I am aware that diabetics and families of diabetics are in every congregation. I realize that knowing how I cope with my disease through my faith might well be of help to some of them. When I am talking about an issue of the faith, and my diabetes provides an appropriate illustration, I do not hesitate to refer to it. On the other hand, I am also aware that Ron Sisk's frustrations and coping mechanisms are not the primary stuff of the gospel. My preaching is not about me. The gospel is about the life and death and resurrection of Jesus Christ and about how this living Christ is available to all of us in our struggles. Any human struggle that distracts significantly from the centrality of Christ in preaching would be more appropriately dealt with in therapy or in some support group than in worship. Yes, Christ cares about us in our struggles. But our struggles are not the point. The good news of Jesus is the point, and we dare not lose sight of that good news.

Still the question remains: what do we do with our preaching when some aspect of our physicality—weight, size, race, gender, sexual orientation, disability, and the like—consumes our energies outside the pulpit? I would argue that the ethics of bringing our physicality into our preaching must center on our gospel purpose. We may refer to our physical issues when, like Paul's thorn, that reference serves the cause of preaching the gospel. A preacher who gets a diagnosis of a terminal illness or the onset of Alzheimer's disease—any condition that will strongly influence the quality of his preaching or the way she is perceived by the congregation—should consult with church leaders and trusted counselors about how and when to make that known to the people. Still, our physical condition is simply not the primary issue for human life. *The* primary issue is our relationship with the God of Jesus Christ. Our physical struggles often affect that relationship. Nonetheless, no preacher should allow herself or himself to be distracted by what is merely a subset of that primary issue. That affirmation, however, moves us to the next logical consideration in the ethics of the preacher's weakness—the preacher's spiritual condition.

Spiritual Health

What does the preacher do when he or she is struggling spiritually? How much should we bring our personal spiritual struggles into our preaching?

In one school of preaching called "confessional preaching," sermons are built around the spiritual journey of the preacher. The late John Claypool, Baptist turned Episcopalian, made confessional preaching his stock-in-trade.[2] Virtually every sermon turned on some aspect of his own journey. Approaching the same idea from a different direction, the great preacher Harry Emerson Fosdick based his preaching on aspects of pastoral care, projecting specific personal issues such as doubt onto the congregation and dealing with them in the sermon. While Claypool in his sermons reflected on his own spiritual health, both of these approaches have enjoyed a good bit of popularity with both preachers and congregations.

Another school of thought is the traditional idea that a preacher should serve as an inspirational spiritual example for the congregation. I know of one preacher in a pietist tradition whose wife and child were killed in an automobile accident. His tradition told him that he should set his congregation an example of how to grieve as a Christian. For him, that meant he should not allow himself to show his pain and loneliness. He later reported to me that one result of his approach, which he thought at the time of his bereavement was quite successful, was that he went into a serious and life-changing depression nearly a quarter of a century later.

Even in circumstances much less dramatic than my friend's sudden bereavement, many preachers simply refuse to carry their personal spiritual struggles into the pulpit with them. To do so feels too personal, too raw, almost exhibitionist. While it is relatively normal even for preachers to question aspects of their faith from time to time, those in the midst of spiritual crises don't usually work out those crises in public. To do so creates a dual burden—a burden for the congregation, which may be ill-equipped to cope with the reality of a perceived flaw in the faith of their spiritual leader, and a burden for the individual to work out his or her issue in a publicly acceptable fashion. Usually preachers in crisis don't want to create either of those burdens. Clearly, one can't avoid communicating aspects of one's spiritual journey and condition in preaching. Those facts are evident to anyone with ears to hear. The most common approach, born primarily of good sense and healthy boundaries, suggests, however, that the preacher should be relatively reluctant to make personal references in sermons. A key mentor of mine maintained that a preacher should refer to himself or herself in sermons in a given year only as many times as there are major holidays in the year.

Emotional Health

The line between spiritual and emotional issues is quite blurry. In the example above of a minister dealing with the death of his wife and child, a spiritual misunderstanding about the appropriate behavior of a pastor in the midst of a personal crisis compounded an emotional difficulty. For all people, depression, anger, and other common emotional issues often have spiritual aspects. For the preacher, however, the question is whether and how to acknowledge those emotions in the pulpit. In preaching, difficulties can arise for both preacher and congregation when a preacher carries into the pulpit some unresolved emotion that either explicitly or implicitly colors the sermon.

Sometimes the emotion is quite explicit. One pastor under whose preaching I sat as a very young man would regularly burst into tears during his sermons. The first few times it happened, I thought he was simply so deeply invested in his subject that it moved him to tears. As time went on, though, I began to realize that the tears often came at odd, even incongruous moments. I ultimately came to the conclusion that this man needed therapy and that his constant imposition of his emotions upon the congregation constituted a kind of abuse. His excessive emotionalism focused our attention on him rather than on what he was saying. Clearly, unresolved issues in his life sat very near the surface, so near the surface, in fact, that he could not consistently control them.

Of course, a preacher may take explicit emotion into the pulpit without even attempting to control it. I have listened to some sermons that came out of the preacher's obvious anger with the congregation over some issue and to others that came from the preacher's anger about issues in the wider world. Recent election cycles have seen many preachers turn their pulpits into venues for venting their personal political frustrations. I talk more about the ethics of political preaching in a later chapter, but for now I will simply say that political venting is clearly out of place in the pulpit.

Paul's advice to the young Timothy seems appropriate as we consider the proper place of emotion in preaching. The apostle appears to counsel that the preacher exercise both moderation and determination. On the one hand, he advises, "Have nothing to do with stupid and senseless controversies; you know that they breed quarrels. And the Lord's servant must not be quarrelsome but kindly to everyone, an apt teacher, patient, correcting opponents with gentleness" (2 Tim. 2:23-25). On the other hand, in perhaps his most famous advice on preaching, Paul counsels, "I solemnly urge you: . . . be persistent whether the time is favorable or unfavorable; convince, rebuke, and encourage, with the utmost patience in teaching" (2 Tim. 4:1-2). To paraphrase, "Don't take your uncontrolled emotions into the pulpit and inflict them on your people. Stay focused on the centrality of the message of Christ and stay passionate about that." Paul wants us both to feel strongly and to express ourselves strongly, but only about matters of central importance.

As Paul's guidance suggests, the wise preacher recognizes the power of emotion and chooses when and how to express it in a sermon. The preacher's personal emotional health is another aspect of this same issue. Is the preacher depressed? Is the preacher unhappy? Are there problems at home? The yardstick for determining whether to bring those issues into the pulpit is the yardstick of the gospel message. If you can help a significant constituency grow in its relationship with Christ, enhancing listeners' personal maturity as believers, by bringing your emotional condition explicitly into the pulpit with you, do so. If you can't, don't.

You bring your emotional condition into the pulpit implicitly whether you want to or not. As a southerner, schooled from the cradle in masking emotions, and as an introvert with a personal horror of revealing things about myself before I am ready to do so, I thought when I became a preacher I would be able to preach without regard to how I was feeling on a given day. I could not have been more wrong. Every congregation has within it people skilled in reading others' emotions. They may not know they can do it, but they somehow instinctively pick up on your facial expressions and body language. Malcolm Gladwell's popular book *Blink!* deals with aspects of this ability and how it comes into play in decision making.[3] In my own experience, time and again, congregants have commented matter-of-factly on emotions I thought I had hidden well. Sometimes they have recognized emotions I didn't even know I was having!

That phenomenon leads us to consider a second, and potentially even more dangerous, way in which our emotional condition can

be expressed implicitly in our preaching. Preachers are by definition passionate people. We preach because we believe. We preach
because we care. For most of us, that caring extends far beyond
the subject of any Sunday-morning sermon. We feel strongly about
politics, about morality, about local and national issues. Those
feelings are important data as we consider what we will say on
a given Sunday. Those feelings are present whether we acknowledge them or not. Unacknowledged, strong feelings can skew a
preacher's work without him or her ever realizing what is going
on. One good idea is to examine your own preaching from time to
time for hidden feelings. Why did you choose one illustration and
not another? Are there subjects that seem to find their way spon-
taneously into the sermon on a regular basis? Do you find yourself
reacting emotionally during a sermon in ways that surprise you or
seem atypical for you? If your answer to any of these questions is
yes, then the cause of that emotional response in your life probably
needs tending.

Relational Health

Two categories need to be considered under the heading of relational health. The first is the pastor's personal and family relationships. The second is the pastor's relationship with the members of
the congregation, either individually or collectively.

To what degree should a pastor bring his or her relationship
with family into preaching? Some things can be said without question. The pulpit is not the place to work on one's marriage or
discipline one's children or take a swipe at a family member who
has irritated you. Your family's right to privacy and confidential-
ity must be respected as much as that of any other member of the
congregation. As a minimal standard, I tell my homiletics classes
that they must never mention a member of their family from the
pulpit without telling that person exactly what they plan to say
and getting that person's permission.

But isn't the life of the pastor's family a part of that pastor's
witness, a part of the substance of her ministry? Of course it is. And
that is precisely why we must be careful to respect the boundaries

of that family relationship. If your family members are not more important to you than your church, if their dignity and privacy are not more important to you than making a point in a sermon (even a very good point that you can't make any other way), then you have misplaced your priorities and seriously compromised your Christian witness.

With proper permission from family members, describing events in your family can provide useful and even entertaining illustrations. Everyone who has ever been married relates to marital stories. Everyone who has ever had a toddler or a teenager knows what that is like. Congregation members like to know that we have the same struggles they do. The key here is not to overdo it. Occasional family references are fine. A steady diet of them transforms your preaching into the My Family show. One possible rule of thumb might be to limit such illustrations to no more than one a month. Certainly, however, if the preacher is dealing with some marital crisis, or some legal or moral issue, that matter should not be subjected to public scrutiny in any form, at least until well after the events themselves (and even then, only with the permission of all involved). If the event is so shattering that it materially affects one's ability to preach or compels immediate disclosure, then the appropriate response for everybody's sake may be to step out of the pulpit until the crisis has passed. The preacher at this juncture might be best advised to seek counsel from the church elders or an ecclesiastical superior, psychologist, or accountability partner.

In one sense, every sermon a preacher delivers is about her relationship with the congregation. That relationship is hardly ever the stated subject of the sermon. But every sermon also helps shape that relationship in one way or another. I have preached when I was proud of the congregation and when I was disappointed in the congregants, when I was grateful and when I was angry, when I was elated and when I was frustrated, when I was seeking to comfort and when I was seeking to challenge. This range of feelings is the stuff of pastoral life.

Of all the various emotions in pastoral life, though, the most destructive to preaching seems to be anger. A pastor who is angry with the congregation and who allows that anger to color his preaching is treading on dangerous ground. Evangelical preachers in America, particularly, have often seemed to confuse prophetic preaching with angry preaching. My wife, who grew up in small congregations in the mountain West, vividly recalls wondering as a child why the preacher was always angry and why he (it was always he) was allowed to yell at them that way. Her experience, I suspect, is more typical than not for a certain genre of congregation.

Whether anger from the pulpit is typical or atypical within a given congregation, however, it is almost always ill-advised. As the apostle James cautions, "Let everyone be quick to listen, slow to speak, slow to anger; for your anger does not produce God's righteousness" (James 1:19-20). A congregation that either feels or thinks the pastor is angry with them may feel guilty, cease attending, construct excuses, get angry in return, or respond in any one of a dozen other possible ways. What people are unlikely to do is improve either their behavior or their relationship with Christ.

Everybody gets angry. Preachers are as liable to that emotion as any other human being. In itself, anger may be a good and healthy emotion. Preachers have a prima facie obligation, however, to deal with their anger in ways that do not infect or corrupt the act of preaching. When a preacher is angry with the congregation, as will inevitably happen, he or she must learn to recognize, express, and deal with that anger in positive and appropriate ways. See a therapist, kick a football, chop wood, pump iron, run a marathon, do whatever you must do so that you don't use God's pulpit as a venue for your venting. If you can't get past your anger with the members, then you can't, or at least you shouldn't, preach to them.

Similarly, the best place to deal with relational issues with an individual member of the congregation is in private. I have some-times seen preachers who were mad at an individual church member or a small group of members use the pulpit to berate unnamed members guilty of the heinous sin of (*fill in the blank*). Part of the problem, of course, is that the people you think need to hear a particular sermon are never there on the Sunday you choose to preach it. Even worse, if they are present, there is a good chance they will see themselves in the story, figure out that you are abusing the pulpit to get at them, and move even further away from the needed reconciliation.

On exceedingly rare occasions, when, for example, you have offended a church member in public, it might be necessary to apologize in public or to assure the congregation that you have done what is necessary for reconciliation. For the most part, however, dealing with these kinds of relational issues from the pulpit seems to me to be both inappropriate and ill-advised. In most congregations, members will come to know that you have patched things up with Deacon Jones in precisely the same way they came to know that you and Deacon Jones were on the outs—by talking about it with one another. Since you can't stop or control such conversation, you might as well allow the church grapevine on occasion to carry some good news along with the usual fare!

How the pastor deals with the issues of his or her own health and the health of his or her relationships constitutes some of the primary data church members use to help themselves decide whether or not they will listen to what you say. Dealing with these issues appropriately helps create a healthy space within which to preach.

CHAPTER 5

All Things to All People

Preaching to a Particular Congregation

The new young preacher at Salt Lick Baptist Church was
having a terrible time getting the congregation off dead
center. The members hated new ideas, and they hated "up-
pity" young seminarians who were always trying to inflict
new ideas upon them. Preacher John was just like all the
rest.

John had just studied in a seminary course on worship
the importance of a church's physical facilities. The little
country sanctuary at Salt Lick had served its congregation
quite well for the past hundred years or so. But since the
addition of electric light around 1930, the church had done
precious little updating of the sanctuary's light fixtures. In
John's opinion, the white clapboard colonial-style building
begged for a central candelabra-type chandelier. So he began to preach in that direction. He talked about the city on
a hill. He talked about the need to care for God's house. He
talked about the old folks who couldn't see as well as they
used to. Finally he announced that at the church business
meeting that week, he would be proposing that the church
spend what for them was an enormous sum, five hundred
dollars, on a new chandelier. You could have heard the
congregation's gasp a mile away.

Naturally, everybody showed up at the business meeting. When the time came, Pastor John stood up and presented his proposal that the church spend five hundred dollars on a new chandelier. He opened the floor for discussion, and the first person to stand and stalk to the lectern was crusty old Deacon Jones. A farmer with dirt under his fingernails and winter in his soul, Deacon Jones was known to brook no nonsense, so nobody was surprised when he said, "Preacher, I'm against this project of yours. It's the worst idea I've ever heard. This church has never had a chandelier. We don't need a chandelier. We don't want a chandelier. We can't afford a chandelier. Why can't you fellas from the seminary ever be practical? What we really need around here is more light!"

We will retire gracefully from the scene of John's failure to communicate in terms his congregation could understand to consider the larger question. What are the ethical considerations a preacher should take into account when preaching to a particular congregation? Is the idiom of preaching a matter of ethics? How should the preacher shape his or her subject matter to meet a particular congregation's needs? What are the considerations when gospel truth and a congregation's cultural or ethical values clash?

The Purpose of Preaching

Clearly, preaching is intended to serve the gospel. Whenever and wherever we preach, our objective is to help people know and follow the God of Jesus Christ. Paul's famous words to the Corinthians serve as a kind of template for helping us consider the ethics of preaching to particular congregations:

> For though I am free with respect to all, I have made myself a slave to all, so that I might win more of them. To the Jews I became as a Jew, in order to win Jews. To those under the law I became as one under the law (though I myself am not under the law) so that I might win those under the law. To those outside the

law I became as one outside the law (though I am not free from God's law but am under Christ's law) so that I might win those outside the law. To the weak I became weak, so that I might win the weak. I have become all things to all people, that I might by all means save some (1 Cor. 9:19-22).

What Paul seems to be saying is that his approach to building relationships with every group entails sensitivity to that group's cultural values and to the way the group perceives reality.

Ethically, the preacher has a prima facie obligation to adjust his approach to the sermon so that it can be heard by those who are listening. In the course of my service as a pastor, for example, I would from time to time be asked to preach to a youth group or to a group of elementary-school-age children. Obviously, I might speak on the same subject that I would address with their parents, but I would never use the same language or the same illustrations. I would try, without making myself ridiculous, to choose vocabulary and illustrations that the youth or children could hear, that were appropriate to their world.

While this principle seems self-evident, even simplistic, most of us only have to think about sermons we have heard to come up with examples of how often the principle is ignored by those who preach. Some theologians have argued that the word of God as embodied in the Scripture speaks for itself to all times and places, and that therefore the preacher should not seek to make preaching relevant to the context. I would argue that such an assertion is a violation of the Scripture itself, at least as Paul and the rabbis understood it. It is precisely the capacity of Scripture to speak to all times and places through the preacher's applications that demonstrates such power in the lives of generations of believers. In his popular introductory text on preaching, Candler professor Tom Long quotes homiletician Leonora Tubbs Tisdale's suggestion that "'preachers need to become amateur ethnographers—skilled in observing and thickly describing the subcultural signs and symbols of the congregations they serve.'"[1] He goes on to affirm that this process is a kind of priestly function, a way the preacher mediates between the people and the Spirit of God. "The preacher goes to the biblical text as a priest, carrying the questions, needs, and concerns of the congregation and world, not as an agenda to be met but as an offering to be made, and then the preacher listens to the text. . . . Whatever that word may be the preacher must tell the truth about it."[2] In effect, Long recognizes the importance of context in the preacher's interpretation of Scripture, but he calls the preacher to speak the truth that is learned whether the congregation wants to hear it or not. For Long every sermon requires a balance between the demand of the gospel and the situation of the congregation.

How deeply must a preacher go into the cultural idiom of her congregation? As deeply as it takes to communicate. The need to communicate appropriately for a congregation's culture is true in subtle ways in every church. When I went as a young man to pastor a church in tobacco-growing rural Kentucky, I had to learn to appropriate the images and rhythms of that farming culture to inform my sermons. Had I not done so, listeners would have been polite, but my sermons would not have penetrated their reality in a meaningful way. California culture presented me with an entirely different communication challenge when I served a church in the Bay Area, as did suburban Fort Worth, Texas, when I served a church there. In this sense, communicating the gospel always entails an element of cultural pragmatism. To communicate you have to be able to speak the language.

Two recent examples help drive home this idea of cultural pragmatism. My colleague Jay Moon recently completed his doctorate in intercultural studies through Asbury Seminary. His dissertation focused on the role of proverbs in the oral culture of the Builsa tribe in Ghana. Moon's thesis was that the way to penetrate an oral culture with gospel beliefs and values is to appropriate suitable aspects of that culture and use them as a way to make the gospel accessible. He worked with the Builsa people, whose oral culture included a large number of proverbs with snippets of wisdom gleaned from the life experiences of that tribe. In working with them, he searched for areas of agreement between the proverbs the Builsa already knew and lived by and aspects of the gospel.[3] For example, he connected the proverb, "When a man is in love, he doesn't count how long and steep the road is to his fiancée's house" with Romans 5:8, "But God proves his love for us in that while we still were sinners Christ died for us." God proves his love by coming to us as a Builsa man proves his love by traveling to his fiancée. The Builsa were able to appreciate the value of demonstrated love.

Randy Woodley, a Native American who is a doctoral graduate of that same intercultural program, is using the same idea to contextualize the gospel for Native Americans in the United States and Canada. Woodley's idea is that the reason the church has failed so abysmally in its efforts to reach Native Americans for Christ is that pastors and missionaries have failed to take into account and appropriate as a part of their communication efforts aspects of Native American culture that already agree with gospel values. For example, he tells the story of one convert who was able to make a commitment to Christianity when he came to view Jesus as the "number one dog soldier." In Native American practice, the dog soldier was the warrior who was willing to give his life to protect the village. These examples share the common theme of contextualization as an ethical value in preaching. The purpose of the sermon must always be to communicate appropriately with the congregation being addressed. By adjusting the expression of the gospel to suit the context, the apostle Paul moved the church into the first great era of Christian missions. Preachers today are called to follow his example.[4]

The Particularity of the Sermon

Long's assertion above that the preacher must speak the truth whether the congregation wants to hear it or not leads us to the next question about the ethics of preaching to a particular congregation. Do a given congregation's cultural, political, and social values mean that a preacher must not address certain subjects or must address them in a certain way, regardless of what the Scripture may actually say on the subject? Certainly that appears to be the case. In the segregated South of my childhood, a preacher who spoke in favor of integrating the public schools was often quite literally taking his life in his hands. In the nominally integrated South of the twenty-first century, a preacher who pushed too hard for organic unity of congregations of different races would run the risk of being viewed as either too radical or irrelevant. In certain congregations, one would not dare to suggest that it might be possible to be homosexual and Christian. In others, one would not dare to suggest that the faith might present objections to homosexual practice. For some, the war in Iraq is a Christian-backed crusade for freedom. For others it is antithetical to Christian values, a disgraceful waste of young lives and the nation's treasure. Either way, preachers, out of sympathy with the majority opinion of the congregation, often find themselves choosing their texts, or at least their illustrations, so as to avoid getting themselves in trouble. Preachers who are personally in sympathy with those majority opinions may find themselves ignoring certain texts and emphasizing others in order to make their point.

Take, for example, biblical teachings with regard to consumption of alcohol. Any serious student of Scripture would have to acknowledge that the witness is ambiguous. On the one hand, Scripture consistently condemns drunkenness and overindulgence. On the other, wine is portrayed as a gift of God intended for human enjoyment. The abstinence tradition in which I grew up consistently ignored positive teachings about alcohol for the sake of making the point about its dangers. Preachers in my tradition often took Paul's caution to the Corinthians regarding meat offered to idols and applied that caution to alcohol, though the passage itself says nothing of the kind. Jesus's turning the water into wine at Cana was never talked about at all, though one was left with the impression that it was viewed as a miracle worker's youthful indiscretion.

Preachers often self-select acceptable topics. The question is, should they? Christian history demonstrates that often the preacher who has taken the risk of saying the unacceptable has made the greatest impact. The Rev. Dr. Martin Luther King Jr. said things no one was supposed to say from a southern pulpit and changed the nation in the process. Bishop Oscar Romero preached contrary to the power structure in El Salvador and was murdered for his trouble. Bishop Desmond Tutu's calls for reconciliation rather than vengeance changed the course of South African history after apartheid. Yet these preachers of courage are notable precisely for being the exception rather than the rule in Christian practice.

In particular situations, Christian preachers, I believe, are called to be aware of the distinction between ordinary time and *kairos* time in Christian teaching. Many of us who preach spend most of our lives in what could legitimately be described as ordinary time. We baptize, we marry, we counsel, we comfort, we bury the people of our congregations. We participate along with them in the life of the community. We preach the ordinary virtues of the Christian life, and for most of us most of the time, that is quite challenging enough. Overall in the Western church, two thousand years of Christian history have forged a culture in which society and the church exist in relative, though often uneasy, harmony.

Inevitably, though, a *kairos* moment comes, a moment when the forces of history and the movement of the Holy Spirit conspire. In those moments, God calls us preachers to challenge the dominant culture, to speak out for change, to take risks in our preaching for the sake of the kingdom. If the congregation supports us in those moments, well and good. If it does not, we are called to preach nonetheless.

I still, of course, haven't answered the question of how you are to know when such a moment has come in your particular situation. Some preachers never seem to stand up for anything that could cause them or anyone else the slightest inconvenience. Others seem to make a career of charging off to tilt at every windmill they can find. As H. Richard Niebuhr wrote in the 1930s, some parts of the church project a vision of the Christ of culture and others of the Christ against culture. Often a cause that engages a portion of the Christian community will leave other portions of that same community indifferent.

There is no magic formula here. Each preacher must seek individual guidance regarding when and how to address a controversial topic. That decision needs to include considerations such as:

- Does this church need to hear about this issue at this moment in its congregational life?

- What gospel purpose will be served by addressing this issue now?
- Will the congregation's culture give listeners "ears to hear"
  what will be said?
- Is speaking out now on this issue a matter of Christian integrity for the preacher, regardless of any consequences?

Even when a denomination or other judicatory has chosen a particular cause for emphasis, every preacher must determine for himself or herself precisely how that emphasis will be carried out in a
given congregation.

Pragmatism in Preaching

We have dealt elsewhere with the question of the preacher's integrity. Here we approach the same issue again from the standpoint of
how one preaches to a congregation with whose culture one may
not be in entire agreement. As a young preacher, I served a church
in Kentucky's tobacco country where residents derived their income
from three primary sources—raising tobacco, breeding racehorses,
and working in the whiskey distilleries. The congregation expected
me to preach against the three "sins" of smoking, gambling, and
drinking, but members also expected to go right on deriving their
income from them. My role as pastor was to conspire tacitly in
the church's essential self-deception. Currently the state of South
Dakota where I live derives a significant portion of its tax income
from video lottery games played at a series of mom-and-pop casinos scattered across the state. Church folk, personally opposed to
gambling, consistently vote to preserve those casinos in order to
protect themselves from the specter of a state income tax. For the
last decade or so, much of the evangelical world has subscribed to
the dictum, "You can't be a Christian and vote Democratic."

Given these cultural realities and a host of others, a preacher's
personal dissent may quickly become a crisis of conscience. Do I
attempt to preach that the abortion issue is more complex than the
cartoonish alternatives with which the extreme positions at either
end of the spectrum have presented us? Do I attempt to lead my

people toward a balanced and reasoned critique of current American foreign policy, or do I simply exercise a kind of neutral chaplaincy? To find answers to questions such as these, the preacher must employ a delicate personal ethical calculus.

First, can a genuine gospel word be heard in this environment? When Jesus told the disciples not to "cast your pearls before swine," he was not saying that people are pigs. What he was saying is that some times and places simply are not conducive to communicating the gospel, and a sensitive preacher learns when to speak and when to keep silent. That does not mean we are ever excused from defending gospel values when they are attacked, but it does mean we need not feel compelled to attempt to make our point when doing so is futile. Missionaries have long known that years of preparatory work are sometimes necessary before people will be ready to hear the gospel. Cultural Christians may have trouble hearing aspects of the gospel too. In some communions here in the United States, seven years into the twenty-first century, people are still not ready to hear that the Bible and science are not in conflict over creation and evolution. Their worldview tells them everything has to be one way or the other. They remain deeply suspicious of any attempt at reconciliation of creation and evolution. In other deeply Christian venues, people would be astonished to hear anything other than that the two perspectives are compatible.

Second, if a genuine gospel word can be heard here, can I find a way to say it? James Michener's novel *Hawaii* includes a marvelous passage in which the missionaries are trying to find a way to translate "Thou shalt not commit adultery" so the native Hawaiians can hear it. The difficulty the missionaries encounter is that the Hawaiian language has several different words for adultery, depending upon the relationship of the partners, while English has only the one word. Finally the missionaries conclude the best translation is, "Thou shalt not sleep mischievously." In a very real sense, the whole of the preaching craft is focused on this process of contextualization, translating the gospel into language the people can hear.

Third, will speaking this gospel word in this context at this time do more good than harm? In one church I served as pastor, I became convinced, as a matter of my own conscience before God, that I knew a set of changes the church needed to make in order to move forward in ministry. My conviction was born of much prayer and of several years' attempts to deal with this situation in a positive fashion, as well as consultation with some experienced and trusted leaders. I was sure I knew what we needed to do, but I was equally sure that speaking that word would create enormous ill will, could very probably split the church, and would almost certainly result in my own dismissal as pastor. I came reluctantly to the conclusion that I could not in good conscience speak that word. The best I could do was find another job, take myself out of the situation, and hope that throwing the system out of balance by leaving would help the people come to a healthy decision on their own. Sometimes you know exactly what needs to be said, and the painful truth is that you are not the one to say it.

Fourth, is this an occasion when conscience and the Holy Spirit lead me to throw caution to the winds and speak regardless of the possible consequences? Even Paul couldn't be all things to all people all the time. He confronted Peter, for example, when he thought the latter was accommodating too much to Jewish practice. The virtues of contextualization have their limits. You reach yours as a preacher when your silence threatens whatever for you is a key gospel value. Would Martin Luther King Jr. have stood up in his church that night in 1955 and advocated the bus boycott if he had known what would happen? Perhaps, but perhaps the real gift of God in these situations is that we don't know. Sometimes we are simply compelled to do what we believe is right and to trust ourselves to the providence of God. Preaching ethically always involves this tension between the pragmatic and the prophetic.

The Pragmatic Cop-out

Other times preachers use pragmatism as an excuse for never confronting evil, never challenging the congregation's cultural and social assumptions at all, but simply going along with prevailing conditions. Unfortunately, one suspects that preachers go along to get along more often than not. Often accommodation becomes the church's besetting sin. That reality, of course, plays out differently in every congregation.

Having spent half my adult life as part of a denomination in the midst of a leadership crisis with serious ethical overtones, I struggled with this issue to some degree in every church I pastored. Do you continue to support a denomination's programs and missions when you disagree strongly with decisions being made? What do you do when members of your congregation are employees of that denomination? Do you speak up when you believe the denomination is incorrectly interpreting Scripture? What do you do when its decisions conflict with what for you is a fundamental moral principle? These questions may seem far-fetched to some, but in my twenty years as a pastor I faced every one of them personally.

I came to the conclusion painfully over time that it is one thing to serve the gospel by becoming all things to all people. It is quite another to forfeit your own integrity in the process. The day came when I had to stand before the members of my congregation and tell them I was leaving that denomination whether they did or not. Some thought I was imprudent for jeopardizing my income. Others thought I was being too hasty, leaping to an unnecessary conclusion. Others thought I was doing harm to the congregation by leading it out of the safety of old relationships and into an uncomfortable new future. Any or all of those criticisms may have been justified. But for me the day came when I had to speak.

The perennial struggle of Christian preachers between what is prudent and what they believe to be right is perhaps exemplified no better than in the famous poem of the German Lutheran pastor Martin Niemöller, written out of his anguish over his early acquiescence to the Nazis. Many versions of the poem are in circulation, but one of the most common goes as follows:

> First they came for the Communists,
> And I said nothing because I wasn't a Communist.
> Then they came for the Jews,
> And I said nothing because I wasn't a Jew.
> Then they came for the trade unionists,
> And I said nothing because I wasn't a trade unionist.
> Then they came for the Catholics,

And I said nothing because I wasn't a Catholic.
Then they came for me,
And by that time there was no one left to speak for me.

Niemöller early changed his stance and became an active op-
ponent of the Nazis, but he struggled all his life with the belief
that he should have spoken up sooner. It is easy enough from the
perspective of history for us to nod our heads sagely and agree
that Niemöller should indeed have done so. It is quite another
thing to be in a particular situation and agonize over what is the
right thing, the best thing to do. In the section above, I gave a set
of criteria for attempting to make such a decision. At this point I
simply acknowledge the difficulty of acting on these suggestions.
Any set of ethical criteria, any template other than the most legalistic, is likely to present the preacher with considerable difficulty
when it comes to deciding whether to speak or not. Just as Joseph
Fletcher's old situation ethics criterion of agape, doing the loving
thing, sounds easy enough but wasn't easy at all in the situations
he outlined in his book, so also any attempt to move from theoretical to practical decision making about when to speak will be
fraught with difficulty.

It is helpful, however, to remember that the same Paul who
sought as a mission strategy to communicate in the language of
every culture he encountered also did not hesitate to confront evil
within the young church whenever he perceived it. Later in the
Corinthian correspondence Paul precipitates a crisis in his relationship with that church by confronting what he regards to be
sinful situations in the personal lives of members and in members'
lack of respect for one another. He does so knowing fully that the
congregation may reject his leadership. Yet he appears to consider
this struggle the very essence of his pastoral responsibility. He says
in 2 Corinthians 2:4, "For I wrote you out of much distress and
anguish of heart and with many tears, not to cause you pain, but
to let you know the abundant love that I have for you." For Paul,
ethical struggle and correction are part and parcel of the pastoral
process. The preacher who doesn't say what needs to be said simply because it isn't easy to say it forgets that preaching isn't supposed to be easy.

CHAPTER 6

For Building Up the Body of Christ

Preaching a Balanced Diet

The regular meeting of the Tuesday morning coffee club at McFriendly's in Silver City was well under way. Getting a discussion started didn't take much. These guys had known each other most of their lives. Farmers and local businessmen, most were members of either First Lutheran or First Methodist Church. Today, as sometimes happened, the discussion turned to recent sermons by Pastor Lars Nelson at First Lutheran and Pastor Jane Fremont at First Methodist.

"I'll tell you one thing," blustered Jack Ferrill. "I'm sick and tired of Pastor Jane preaching about money. Ever since we started this new building program, it's been money, money, money with her. You start to think that's all the Bible's about."

"Now, Jack," responded Tim Elway, who had been calming Jack down ever since they were in high school. "It could be worse. My friend Joe over at the Baptist church says all they're getting these days is 'Witness! Witness! Witness!' You'd get sick of that real fast. And Pastor Edwards over at Second Assembly has been on the book of Revelation for six months to my certain knowledge. My sister goes there, and it's all she can talk about."

"Huh," snorted Fred Nelson, the oldest member of the group. "With Pastor Lars it's always grace—grace this and grace that. I'd like to hear about responsibility for a change. The Ten Commandments was the text last week. Darned if he didn't talk about them as vehicles of grace. Don't these guys learn how to preach in seminary?"

The discussion went on through three cups of coffee and at least two orders apiece of miniature cinnamon rolls, but you get the idea. Church folk pay more attention to our sermons than those of us who preach think they do. They have an intuitive sense of what a balanced diet of preaching is, and thoughtful parishioners know when they are not getting it. Ethically, preachers have an obligation to build up the body of Christ. We are to do good and not harm. We need to approach our preaching as a sacred task designed to help all those who listen to us grow in their understanding of the gospel, their commitment to Christ, and their service for Christ in the church and the world. The question for this chapter is, how do you and I conceptualize and deliver a balanced diet of preaching for our congregations? We will begin with a look at what is not a balanced diet in contemporary preaching. Next we will explore a bit about the relationship between your core theology and the subject matter of your preaching. Then we will look at some practical suggestions for shaping your preaching in what this preacher at least considers to be a balanced way.

Preaching as Fast Food

One of the most significant problems in American church life in the early years of the twenty-first century is that the preaching diet too many believers are being fed from week to week fails to address the depth and breadth of Christian formation. The American success ethic has driven preachers to build their churches by concentrating on reaching particular segments of the "market" with targeted preaching. For example, in recent years we have seen the development of many seeker-oriented churches. These churches succeed by targeting an essentially unchurched segment of the population, people without a church background who are looking for meaning in life. These congregations focus on helping secular people learn and commit to the basics of the Christian faith. They are often very good at helping people through the first year or two of their Christian life. They are not often as good at helping new Christians become mature believers. Other congregations in the "marketplace" may attempt to distill the gospel to a dominant idea, such as the "Your Best Life Now" approach of popular preacher Joel Osteen. Previous generations heard this approach in Norman Vincent Peale's "power of positive thinking" or Robert Schuller's "possibility thinking" or Billy Graham's focus on an initial commitment to Christ. Graham, of course, wasn't attempting to build a congregation, but the others were, and their "brand identity" helped them. They became successful by providing an easily recognized "product," a particular focus in preaching. In effect, they were providing theological fast food.

The dark side to this approach is that it can and often does lend itself to charlatanism. Preachers of the prosperity gospel, bogus faith healers, feel-good merchants, and a host of others have used the trappings of Christianity to disguise their own quests for money and power. In so doing, they have often left out the essential nourishment of the historic Christian faith. But these extremes are merely the most egregious examples of the problem. Any approach that does not at some point present the core Christian doctrine of salvation by grace through faith in Jesus Christ can be fairly described as heresy.

Lack of balance in preaching, though, and the consequent danger of malnourishment for believers is not limited to charlatans. Denominations, while broadly orthodox, tend to emphasize certain theological themes as part of their tradition. Lutherans do talk a lot about grace, just as the Baptist churches of my childhood emphasized the moment of decision. Nazarenes talk about Christian perfection. Pentecostals major in the Holy Spirit. Theological questions aside, there is nothing wrong with emphases that help give definition and shape to a congregation's message. They are not fast food as such. To extend the metaphor, perhaps a bit too far, they are more like a distinctive sauce, flavoring all the offerings on a given congregation's menu.

The difficulty with a particular theological emphasis in preaching arises any time a single idea or a truncated cluster of ideas is allowed to dominate the actual Sunday-by-Sunday preaching of a given congregation. I have known preachers who were so focused on conversion that they seemed to have nothing else to say. Once they got everybody in the congregation saved, all they could do was start over and try to get them all saved again! Some churches preach only social justice. Some major in eschatology. Others focus their attention on one side or the other in particular controversies such as abortion or homosexuality. The danger in this reductionism is that no single theme is ever adequate to convey the full richness of the gospel.

While many church folk may be discerning enough to recognize that something is wrong in the diet they are getting from the pulpit, many won't have the theological expertise to recognize exactly what that problem is or how to counteract it. They may end up thinking that this limited perspective on the gospel they are hearing is a full diet, and they themselves are somehow wrong. Or they may simply reject the faith altogether.

Despite its initial appeal to those whose faith is immature, ultimately no simplistic, partial version of the faith proves satisfying over time, any more than a diet made up exclusively of french fries and chocolate milkshakes builds strong bodies. Preachers need to think carefully about the kind of gospel diet their preaching provides.

Preaching as Theological Fare

In an earlier chapter I explored the interaction between a preacher's theological beliefs and his or her preaching. Preaching your own theology accurately is a matter of ethical integrity. In this section, however, I want to look at *how* your theology shapes the range of subject matter in your pulpit offerings. You may not be providing homiletical fast food but still not be providing a balanced homiletical diet.

In her book *Christianity for the Rest of Us: How the Neighborhood Church Is Transforming the Faith*,[1] researcher Diana Butler

Bass writes about how many churches in mainline Protestantism are reinventing themselves. Bass observes that these congregations have a new emphasis on spirituality as a corrective for earlier practices. The social liberalism of the 1960s lacked an emphasis on spiritual experience. The effect of that lack was that many in the church forgot the spiritual underpinnings of their social concern. She hastens to say that these churches are no less liberal than they were. Through their new efforts, they simply seek to provide a more holistic vision of the faith. They are creating new communities to replace the traditional communities lost in the social upheavals that contributed to the decline of mainline Protestantism in the mid-twentieth century. To invigorate these new communities, they are dealing with more personal aspects of the gospel message. At the other end of the theological spectrum from Bass's work, churches that once focused solely on conversion also find new energy as they challenge their congregants to meaningful Christian service. They are no less evangelical, but they are becoming more socially aware.

These changes in emphasis at both ends of the American theological spectrum represent the tendency for the church over time to self-correct its homiletical and theological missteps. The theological stream that once preached only social action is realizing Christians still need a personal spiritual home, a reason for what they do. And the theological stream that once preached only conversion is realizing converted people are called to do something for others as a result of that conversion. Preaching in these congregations follows the flow of these changes in theological emphasis.

If, as the title of this chapter suggests, the apostle Paul was correct that the task of the preacher is building up the body of Christ, equipping the saints for the work of ministry (Eph. 4:7-16), then these trends in the American church may represent the church's recognition of the importance of that task. Every preacher goes about building up the church differently. Every tradition has its own particular emphases. *But every sermon needs to have the goal of strengthening the church and equipping the saints.* Sermons should both help people understand the Christian life and encourage them to live it. That task is part of the biblical ethical imperative for the preacher.

Working from my own theological background in the Baptist tradition, I set forth below touch points that taken together make a preacher's offerings a balanced diet—evangelism, Christian ethics, pastoral care, church practice, and church doctrine and history. Your touch points, working from your tradition, may well be very different. These emphases are not intended as a rigid prescription. Rather, they represent the contours of a healthy preaching diet in normal times in a church of my own tradition. Note that I assume that every sermon is based on a guiding biblical text. While some homileticians and some traditions believe differently, I stand with those who argue that a true sermon must somehow grow out of conversation with the text.

Evangelism

The vast majority of the Baptist tradition espouses a conversionist theology. Baptists believe that people must come to Christ individually by decision. Evangelistic preaching is supposed to provide people with the story of what Jesus has done for us and instructions for how to appropriate that salvation for oneself. (My mother's birth tradition, the Primitive Baptists, by contrast, do not believe the church should evangelize. They espouse a hyper-Calvinism that believes God will save the heathen when and if God chooses.) This theological emphasis on evangelism has found its way into Baptist preaching in a number of ways, some healthy and some not so healthy.

By healthy in this context I mean preaching that is nonmanipulative and that respects people's right of free choice. At the healthier end of the spectrum is a genuine concern for telling the gospel story in ways that appeal to ever-expanding constituencies. At the less healthy end is a tendency to focus every sermon on that initial decision to follow Christ as though life were one big Billy Graham revival. (Note: This is not a criticism of what Graham has done. His has been a specialized ministry, not a local congregation.) The Christian life involves a great deal more than that initial decision. Some preachers also feel compelled to tack on a call to conversion to every sermon, whether what they are doing is a communion meditation for the church, a Christmas Eve devotional, or a funeral service for an infant. Such addenda may or may not be appropriate in a given situation.

The danger with an overemphasis on initial conversion is that it trivializes what it means to live as a converted person. Conversion is a lifelong process, and most Christians experience that converting life as a long, slow growth in their maturity as believers. Always focusing on the drama of initial conversion tends to make people doubt the importance of everyday Christian growth. Because they are not dramatically more devout or more virtuous people than they were last year, they start to question the validity of their conversion. Being baptized two or three times, a practice that in many traditions would be viewed as heresy, is not at all unusual in some Baptist circles.

In a healthy Baptist diet, then, conversion would be a regular but not exclusive pulpit emphasis. My own practice as a pastor was to focus on initial conversion as a topic every six weeks or so. I would encourage church members to invite their unconverted friends for those Sundays. And I would offer in every sermon a picture of relationship with the risen Christ that could be appealing to those searching for answers to their spiritual questions.

Christian Ethics

A second major emphasis in Baptist preaching is the education of the congregation about how one lives a Christian lifestyle. This area of preaching includes various ethical topics, from the Ten Commandments to the culture wars. On the one hand, preaching about piety is an important, even necessary part of a balanced preaching diet. People need to know that Christians don't steal, that truth telling and marital fidelity are basic Christian virtues. Much can be gained from Sunday sermons every few weeks focusing on aspects of Christian ethical behavior.

The danger in this category of preaching occurs when a preacher seizes upon one or two ethical issues, elevates them to primacy, and repeatedly makes those issues the text or subtext of her preaching. At one time in Baptist life, you could count on hearing the subject of alcohol consumption addressed from a typical pulpit every couple of weeks. Many American pulpits have been

dominated in recent years by the issues of abortion and homosexuality. African American pulpits sometimes become focused on
issues related to civil rights. Ethical issues may be important and
worthy of attention. But no single ethical issue, emphasized by
itself, can bear the whole weight of the gospel message. Whether
one holds the "right" or "wrong" position on abortion does not
determine whether one can receive salvation. Nor does any other
form of political correctness or works righteousness.

Rather, the Christian preacher, always mindful of both the reality of grace and the call to obedience, seeks to present the ethical
standards of the faith regularly and compassionately to encourage
people to grow in their commitment to shape their lives according
to gospel values. The preacher can rotate emphases on particular
ethical issues so that the congregation over time receives a relatively comprehensive picture of the nature of Christian ethical life.

Sometimes, of course, an ethical issue rises to the surface of
national awareness or becomes a political issue (more about this
later), and the preacher is tempted to focus on the subject extensively. Two cautions are in order here. First, when people are upset, trying to have a meaningful discussion is never helpful. That is
the time for listening, not pronouncements. Second, these controversial issues have tended in recent years to become politicized and
highly partisan. White-hot political issues seldom lead to meaningful Christian dialogue. In the Baptist tradition, the separation of
church and state is considered absolute, precisely to protect the
integrity of the pulpit. I discuss all of this more fully in the chapter
on political preaching.

Pastoral Care

People have difficult lives. They need the comfort, understanding,
and counsel that a balanced Christian perspective on life can provide them. Death, illness, crisis, tragedy, and the daily demands
of work and family all need to be dealt with from the pulpit on a
regular basis. Often the seeker churches of the past twenty years
have focused almost exclusively on helping people help themselves
as a means of building their congregations. Sunday sermons tend
to bear titles such as "Six Hints for Disciplining Your Child." They

end up being light on Scripture and heavy on pop psychology. Many churches have been highly successful with this approach.

Although the Bible is about the encounter of flawed human beings with the spirit of God and the person of Jesus Christ, it is not a self-help book with a series of neat formulas for successful living in the twenty-first century. To the extent that the story of that encounter illuminates everyday problems, pastoral-care preaching can be very helpful indeed. At the same time, worship is not intended to be either group therapy or a series of how-to classes. Virtually any sermon from a Christian pulpit will include elements of pastoral care. It may also include specific suggestions for healthy Christian behaviors. That care comes in part from the Scripture and in part from the ongoing pastoral relationship of the preacher with the people. But to focus only or even primarily on pastoral care concerns is to run the risk of preaching a truncated prosperity gospel. Some therapeutic and how-to sermons may be very helpful in specific situations. Still, one does not become a Christian in order to get rich, be successful, and feel good about oneself. One becomes a Christian in order to live life in relationship with the God of Jesus Christ.

When twenty-first-century Baptist preachers emphasize this kind of preaching, they seem to do so largely as part of a quest for large numbers of converts. The danger is that they will cultivate believers who commit themselves to the church solely or primarily for "what I can get out of it." A balanced preaching diet also challenges Christians to give of themselves in service to others. As with the first two emphases, pastoral-care preaching is a regular but not exclusive part of a balanced preaching diet.

Church Practice

By church practice I mean the various elements that make up the life of a contemporary congregation—everything from financial stewardship to Christian service to vision casting to denominational emphases to national holidays. In addition, liturgical churches see the festivals of the Christian year as foundational in the way the church communicates and lives out the gospel story. Preachers often feel compelled to interpret church practices for the congregation, and in this context, the Bible often becomes a lens for viewing the institutional life of the church. Clearly, church practice needs to be addressed in preaching because people need to understand what the church is doing and why. Sometimes, though, even church practice can be emphasized too much for a healthy balance in preaching.

In the introductory homiletics course I teach, I use part of one period to challenge students to name every annual special emphasis they can think of from their tradition. It is a fascinating hour. Students quickly come up with long, long lists of emphases. Often there are more yearly emphases on their lists than there are Sundays in a calendar year. While the branch of the Baptist tradition in which I was raised did not follow the Christian year as such (although some do), even there we scarcely had a week when something being stressed in the community, the church, or the denomination was not referred to from the pulpit. I can remember one Sunday as a pastor when I needed to come up with a sermon appropriate to the fall Sunday-school kickoff, the dedication of the new organ, and the annual stewardship campaign all at once. Try to find a text for that one!

The wise preacher resists becoming too programmatic in his or her preaching. Preaching must always keep in mind the whole gospel story rather than allow itself to become too caught up in the minutiae of church practice. By that I do not mean, as some would suggest, that you should never, for example, preach about money. Jesus spoke more about the spiritual and ethical aspects of financial matters than he did about any other single subject. Preaching a balanced diet doesn't mean you can't deal with specifics.

The difficulty here, though, involves how we are perceived as preachers. Parishioners often see preaching about programmatic, institutional matters as an especial exercise in self-interest for a pastor. "Of course she preaches about money. She wants us to raise her salary." With today's inherent suspicion of institutions, church folk, rightly or wrongly, are quick to infer unworthy motivation in what we say. Sermons about Christian service may be seen as attempts to prop up the church's programs. Sermons about the church's polity may be seen as grabbing for power.

This issue becomes especially difficult when the church is in a building program. Church leaders will usually see the success of the program as a major part of the church's agenda. They will want the preacher to address it. But if people perceive that the building program is "all going to church here is about," they will react very negatively. One particular difficulty for preachers is that issues on our minds tend to work their way into our sermons, whether they are the primary subject of the sermon or not. People are very good at picking up on what we believe to be clever programmatic asides. And they are quick to deduce that these asides represent what we are really concerned about. Unfortunately, they are usually right. I remember my wife, exasperated, telling me at one point, "Stop preaching about the church. I'm sick of it. I want to hear about Jesus!" She is a very wise woman.

Church Doctrine and History

Every church tradition has its own historical, doctrinal, and theological emphases. For Baptists those emphases have tended to include the necessity of salvation through personal relationship with Jesus Christ, the insistence upon believer's baptism by immersion, the idea that the individual believer is competent to work out his or her own relationship with God (soul competency), the priesthood of the believer, the autonomy of the local church, and the importance of holy living. They tend to find their way into the pulpit in regular series of sermons on Baptist beliefs. More common to Baptist preaching, they undergird each Sunday's sermon, serving as a conceptual framework, a worldview within which the faith is interpreted. In the same way, my Lutheran students frequently quote Luther to confirm their homiletical points or offer some aside about Lutheran ways.

One of the preacher's duties is always to teach the congregation how its tradition approaches the faith. In an age when denominationalism seems to be on the wane, listeners may well need doctrinal preaching more than ever. However, as with the other subject areas I have mentioned, some preachers emphasize doctrinal preaching almost to the exclusion of other subjects. In the

Midwest where I live, whole churches have been started in recent years to emphasize particular views of Calvinism or eschatology.

Therefore, like an insistent cadence on the march to Zion (an obscure Baptist hymn reference—never mind if you don't get it), I come back to the point of balance. Some doctrinal preaching does help church folk develop a more mature faith. Too much encourages them to live in their heads, devalue other understandings of the faith, and turn Christian belief into a search for doctrinal purity. The story is told of Roger Williams, founder of the first Baptist church in America in Providence, Rhode Island, that he worshiped with that congregation for only a couple of months. He decided it was not doctrinally pure enough, so he began to worship in his home with just his family and a few select friends. Then he decided the others in the group weren't pure enough, so he began to worship with his wife alone. Ultimately he decided her doctrinal views were too impure as well, so he ended up worshiping out in the woods alone! Apocryphal or not, that story suggests the very real danger in a faith focused exclusively on doctrinal purity.

Preaching as Optimum Nourishment

One could offer a number of theological criticisms of the sample Baptist preaching diet I have laid out above. My guess is that you, dear reader, are already doing so. For example, the diet suggested above seriously neglects the spiritual disciplines. But that is not the point. The point of the exercise is to encourage you to think about what does constitute an optimum preaching diet from your own tradition and point of view. Choose five to eight key areas that you believe you need to emphasize regularly, given your own best understanding of the faith. Then shape your preaching according to those touch points.

If we do not give careful thought to the staples of the preaching diet we offer the congregations we serve, then we inevitably allow ourselves to become subject to our own prejudices, the circumstances of the moment, causes célèbres, or the programmatic details of church life. The preacher's pseudo-pious argument that he prefers simply to "let the Spirit lead" week to week works out in many cases to be little more than an excuse for laziness. Instead, we need to give the Spirit an opportunity to work through our planning.

One practical way to address providing balance, once we have decided on the general content of the diet we wish to provide, is to plan the general topics for a year's preaching. For those who don't like to think in such large blocks, the same kind of planning could be done quarterly. Quarterly planning also allows the preacher to correct in the future quarter any perceived deficiencies in subject matter from the quarter just past.

Another key to providing the congregation with an optimum preaching diet on an ongoing basis is to regularly and ruthlessly analyze what you are currently delivering. Keep a list of your topics and texts, and go over that list from time to time, asking yourself whether that list falls in line with the overall guidelines you have chosen. Accustom yourself to the spiritual discipline of self-examination. We all care about some things more than others. Any of us may from time to time get on a hobbyhorse and ride it into the ground. We owe it to the congregations we serve to be honest with ourselves and with God about whatever ideas or topics may be engaging our focus and to ask whether we are attempting to meet their needs or our own.

The goal in seeking to balance our preaching is exactly what is stated in the title of this chapter—building up the body of Christ. The goal is the spiritual health of the congregation as a whole and of the members of the congregation as individuals. As preachers we lose sight of that goal to the peril of the church.

CHAPTER 7

Study to Show Yourself Approved

Preaching What You Know

Sunday morning in Kansas. Nancy Maynard knew it was going to be another bad day at church as soon as she drove into the lot and saw the topic for the sermon on the church marquee. As the science teacher at the local high school, she had been cringing regularly in worship ever since the preacher got embroiled in the state legislature's debate over teaching evolution. Pastor John was a dyed-in-the-wool six-day creationist, and he made no bones about that regularly and emphatically from the pulpit at St. Luke's.

What bothered Nancy most was the way John consistently misrepresented scientific theory from the pulpit. He seemed to have bought in completely to the arguments of that loudmouth on the afternoon Christian radio talk show. He quoted the DJ frequently and at length. The problem was that neither John nor the DJ was a trained scientist. They might be trained in theology (although Nancy seriously doubted the DJ was), but it never took more than a sentence or two before it became clear to anyone who knew about evolutionary theory that John had no idea what he was talking about.

Nancy herself had reconciled her faith and her profession long ago. As a college student she had come to believe that Scripture and scientific theory were talking about different but not mutually exclusive views of reality. Scripture spoke poetically about the origins of creation in the mind of God. For Nancy that wasn't a problem. Science, she knew, simply drew provisional inferences from observation of the material world. She just couldn't see why people were getting so upset about teaching the kids scientific theory.

What really bothered her, though, was the way she was feeling about everything Pastor John said from the pulpit as a result of his crusade against evolution. If he was so sloppy in doing his research on evolutionary theory and the principles of science, she wondered what else he was preaching as fact without checking things out beforehand. Didn't a preacher have an obligation to stick to subjects he or she knew? What was he saying to her children when Nancy wasn't present? Could she really trust him as spiritual leader for her family? Sighing and putting on her Sunday smile, Nancy herded the kids toward the church door. As she did, though, she found herself wondering how much longer she would be able to do this.

Those who summarize American history tell us there was a day when theology was considered the queen of the sciences and the preacher was the most educated person in town. That day is long gone. The proliferation of knowledge of every kind has made it increasingly difficult for anyone to know it all, despite the *Encyclopaedia Britannica* and the comic writer Bill Bryson's *A Short History of Nearly Everything*. The preacher's effective area of expertise has become more and more limited at the same time that the preacher's role as interpreter of the meaning of life for the congregation has become ever more important in a complex and confusing world.

The question is, how does a preacher give a congregation meaningful help in dealing with crucial life issues without at the same time implicitly or explicitly claiming to know more than she or he actually does? In this chapter we will examine the ethics of preaching what you know and what you don't know.

The preacher comes into the pulpit with what in most people's minds is a fairly well-defined area of expertise. However our tradition defines it, we are expected to have a personal relationship with the God of Jesus Christ. We are expected to know the Scripture. We are expected to know the theology of our particular tradition and how that compares to the theologies of the traditions around us. We are expected to know a great deal about human nature (read *sin*—our own and others'). And we are expected to be reasonably well informed on current events and how the faith speaks to a Christian perspective on those events. When people listen to us preach, they begin by assuming that in these arenas at least, you and I will know what we are talking about.

The reality, of course, is a good bit spottier than the paragraph above suggests. Some of us studied the original languages of the Scriptures extensively in seminary. More of us took the required courses and stopped right there. Some of us have extensive training in psychology while others don't. If we came to the ministry from another career, we carry that old body of expertise with us, and, for many of us, that experience in business or education or farming becomes an additional interpretive filter for our theological opinions. For some of us, these other experiences in life may be as influential as our ministerial training in shaping what we say. And then, of course, we have our personal interests. Some of us hate sports and love politics. Some of us love sports and hate politics. In short, none of us is as theologically or experientially well-rounded as we like to think or, for that matter, as the church may assume.

The Scriptures

Ethically, the preacher comes to the sermon with a prima facie obligation to interpret Scripture as correctly as possible, given her education and perspective. Because the Christian Scriptures are viewed theologically as living, in the sense that the Spirit of God speaks through them to those who read and study the Bible, there is a sense in which any scriptural interpretation is always provisional and incomplete. The same lectionary passage, chosen for the same Sunday in the church year, may speak very differently to the pastor of a one-hundred-member African American congregation in

Kentucky and the pastor of a two-thousand-member senior adult congregation in Florida. It may say something very different to the same preacher when it comes up again in the cycle three years later.

Nonetheless, as much as is humanly possible, our job is to get it right. That means, scholar or not, every pastor every week needs to make every possible effort to discover the full meaning of a passage in its context and to think carefully about how that meaning may apply to the congregation that is to hear the sermon.

In addition, the preacher has an obligation to study how others both within the preacher's tradition and outside it have interpreted and used that passage in the past. If a passage has usually been interpreted one way, then we may still come up with a valid new interpretation, but we need to be very careful about declaring ourselves to be right and the rest of Christian tradition wrong. The Wesleyan quadrilateral, a Christian decision-making method attributed to John Wesley, seems a useful tool here. That rubric suggests that authority for the church is found in the conversation between Scripture, tradition, personal experience, and reason. My own Baptist tradition tends to insist that authority comes only from the Scripture. In practice, what that usually means is that the other elements of the quadrilateral find their way into making decisions on matters of faith and practice just as much as they would for Methodists but without appropriate awareness or acknowledgment. The preacher who seeks an accurate interpretation of a passage is well advised to study how the church has interpreted a passage, how it has not, and what historical and social factors contributed to the interpretive choices that were made.

Potential for a major ethical pitfall pops up whenever a preacher has a strong personal investment in citing scriptural sanction for a particular position he or she wishes to take in a sermon. Sometimes the Bible does say precisely what we want it to say. Sometimes it does not. Witness, for example, the long-held Southern Baptist assertion that the Bible says Christians should not drink alcohol. The Scripture does not, in fact, say precisely that. It does suggest extreme caution, but it does not say what generations of temperance workers have wished it did. Nor does the Bible say precisely what a lot of folk would like it to say about abortion or capital punishment or a host of other issues. Often the Bible appears to contradict itself on issues or speaks with more than one voice. The preacher who fudges by suggesting that the Bible says what it does not for the sake of argument does incalculable damage both to his or her own integrity and to the church's perception of that integrity.

As important as not saying what the Bible does not say is honesty about those things the Bible does say, whether we like what it says or not. The Bible is a book of its own time and culture. It, for example, has some very direct and specific things to say about divorce that run counter to interpretation and practice in most Christian communions in America in the twenty-first century. A preacher may wish to argue that those passages are no longer applicable or authoritative. Those arguments can be made. But we should be very careful indeed about arguing that the Scripture doesn't actually say what it does plainly appear to say. To argue that Jesus didn't say that divorce is allowable only in the case of infidelity, when the Gospel according to Matthew clearly quotes him as saying that (19:9), tends to undermine faith both in the Scriptures and in the preacher.

The preacher has an obligation to help educate the congregation in how to interpret the Scripture so that over time people can learn to read Scripture better for themselves. During my own seminary studies thirty years ago, it was not at all uncommon to hear students say things like, "I can't tell my church what this passage means. They'd fire me!" In effect, they meant that they dared not invite people to rethink traditional interpretations in light of ones they were learning based on more recent scholarship. So it was not at all unusual, for example, to hear a student who could speak eloquently in class about the assembling of the Hebrew canon also preach the creation story as though Eden were an address in Mesopotamia.

Thoughtfully teaching the congregation becomes a crucial part of the preacher's task. On the one hand, we don't want to shock people. But on the other hand, neither do we want people to remain ignorant of better interpretations simply because it is difficult to challenge traditional assumptions. Gently, when it is appropriate, the preacher needs to help people understand that the discipline of biblical scholarship opens up the Scripture for us in ways that make it even more appropriate and applicable to our world than simplistic literalism could ever do. By way of caution, Karl Barth says, "Biblical criticism in the pulpit . . . falls under the need for tact. It should be introduced only in the context of ministry and done with respect, not under the pressure of a false ideal of truthfulness."[1] If we bring people along gently, they will listen and they will learn.

Finally, Barth reminds us that the preacher must bring a certain modesty to the task of interpretation. Barth says:

> The gospel is not in our thoughts or hearts; it is in scripture. The dearest habits and best insights that I have—I must give them all up before listening. I must not use them to protect myself against the breakthrough of a knowledge that derives from scripture. Again and again I must let myself be contradicted. I must let myself be loosened up. I must be able to surrender everything.[2]

Precisely because she is herself constantly under scriptural critique, in conversation with and submission to the text, the preacher has something worthwhile to say. Scripture challenges our assumptions and calls us to change. In changing ourselves we gain the ability to speak about change to our listeners.

Everything Else

The Scriptures are the primary area of the preacher's expertise. The next question, though, is what other knowledge do you have to offer in your preaching? Barth and many evangelical theologians would tend to argue that the preacher should restrict herself to Scripture—that the text itself is the contribution the church has to make to the contemporary world. Others would say that the text pushes us to apply the gospel to all of life.

Either way, the preacher encounters an ethical problem. How do I make sure that what I say about any subject from the pulpit is accurate and appropriate for inclusion within a Christian sermon? The proliferation of source material with the growth of the

Internet and other media makes this problem even more difficult. Wikipedia, for example, that online pooling of knowledge from volunteer contributors, certainly purports to be accurate and authoritative by virtue of its openness to correction from any quarter. But there is no objective agent of verification for the content of specific articles.

Similarly, much of contemporary Christian preaching in America is suffused with information the preacher has heard on "Christian" radio or gleaned from publications such as *Time, Newsweek, The Christian Century,* or *Christianity Today.* While these are the very sources (with the exception of "Christian" radio and television!) that homiletics professors like me counsel our students to consult, it is crucial to remember that every source—spoken and written and video, in print or online—has an editorial perspective. Assertions quoted as factual may or may not be so. What is considered accurate at a given moment or from a particular perspective may be called into question by the next piece of research or a different perspective.

What, then, is a preacher to trust as a source for his or her study and assert as an authority when she or he speaks? One could end up, as some do, afraid ever to say anything for fear of getting it wrong or, at the other extreme, willing to credit any source, no matter how dubious, out of frustration with the difficulty of knowing for sure. How does a preacher approach the search for reliable information?

First, it is important to acknowledge that, in a sense, all knowledge in this life is limited and provisional. We may be absolutely sure we are right and yet be absolutely wrong. So the assertions we make are assertions of faith. We may believe that evolution is a description of the creation process. We may believe based on the evidence we have that life begins at a particular moment in time, although which moment is in considerable dispute. We may believe that nuclear energy is a dangerous source of pollution or the potential agent of salvation for the nation's energy needs. But many things we will know absolutely only when God chooses to set us straight.

Second, owning that she must be modest about her certainties, the preacher seeks to develop a list of sources and authorities that she deems trustworthy. These will be sources that are regular touch points to be consulted as issues arise. Many preachers choose a favorite newspaper such as *The New York Times* or *The Wall Street Journal*. They may read a favorite newsmagazine or watch a favorite news analysis program on TV. Some pay attention to particular columnists. Methodist preachers use the *Book of Discipline* and the pronouncements of the annual conference as guidelines of ecclesiastical authority. Virtually every denomination, hierarchical or congregational, has some locus of authority.

The key is to recognize that your assumptions and your conclusions are shaped by the sources you consult. As a conservative Christian and a liberal Democrat, I need to read sources that challenge my assumptions as well as sources that support my assumptions. You need to read broadly too, no matter what your theology and political philosophy may be. I also need to recognize that the fact that I believe a thing is true may not necessarily mean that it is demonstrably true enough for me to assert from the pulpit. The standard for facts and assumptions to be preached goes well beyond that for ordinary conversation.

Third, when I do make a factual assertion from the pulpit, I need to be willing and able to cite the source upon which I base that assertion. That does not mean that a sermon needs to be a series of footnotes. It does mean that the preacher needs to know where he got his facts and whether those facts are or are not in dispute. If you publish your sermons, it may be helpful to include citations of sources for matters that are not common knowledge.

Fourth, a corollary idea is that many sermons should not be preached without considerable research by the preacher. In this day when sermons address everything from the legal status of immigrants to the perils of climate change, it is incumbent upon the preacher to seek out and cite reliable and authoritative sources. These sources may be as varied as the subjects for preaching themselves. They may purport to be impartial or be highly partisan. The preacher's job is to recognize the biases in the information he or she receives and either filter out biased information or make those biases clear when the information is spoken from the pulpit.

One of the sermons I show my introductory homiletics class was done several years ago by the United Methodist preacher Adam

Hamilton during the controversy over the teaching of evolution in Kansas schools. As he begins that sermon, Hamilton takes several minutes to show the congregation the sources from both sides of the issue that he read in preparation for the sermon. Those sources went all the way from the text of the proposed legislation itself to Charles Darwin's *The Origin of Species*. Because he was going to adopt a particular perspective, Hamilton thought it only fair to let the congregation know how he arrived at that perspective. Not the least of the facts that he shared was his own training as a biologist. Note that Hamilton is clearly not the Pastor John of the opening vignette!

Boundaries

So far, I have said that the preacher is obligated to research both scriptural and secular sources carefully, to avoid taking as factual that which comes from biased sources, and to be willing and able to cite the sources for the assertions he or she makes from the pulpit. The question the approach I have outlined raises is, are there limits on the subjects a preacher should attempt?

As I said above, the preacher's primary area of expertise is Scripture and the application of Scripture to life. With the classic preacher George Buttrick of an earlier generation, I would argue that the only true sermon is a biblical sermon. If, in other words, no guiding text can be found for consideration of a given subject, then by biblical criteria the subject itself would be unsuitable for preaching. A clever preacher, of course, can almost always find a text with which to frame virtually any subject. The deeper question then becomes whether this particular use of the text is faithful to the purpose for which the text was written. Scripture addresses the human condition, and biblical sermons should do the same.

Let's say, for example, that the preacher wishes to write a sermon on the phenomenon of global warming and the human response to it. Human stewardship of the environment clearly falls within the purview of Christian teaching. No texts address the phenomenon of global warming explicitly, but plenty of texts consider human stewardship of God's creation.

Perhaps, though, the preacher wants to analyze precisely what causes global warming. Here he has entered the realm of scientific theory. He can quote what others say, but, absent a degree in environmental science, he is unlikely to have the expertise to comment authoritatively. Any preacher in this situation would be far better off to confine her remarks to what Scripture does say rather than to venture into areas she does not understand.

But let's consider a more difficult example. Take the subject of clinical depression. Certainly depression is alluded to in Scripture. From Job on the dung heap to the writer of Ecclesiastes to Elijah in the wilderness, biblical characters got depressed and had to deal with their feelings. Nor is depression a stranger to congregations today. Life is difficult, and many people struggle mightily with feelings of worthlessness, sadness, and meaninglessness. So it seems as though depression would be a perfect subject for the preacher to address.

But it is not that simple. Students of medicine in general and psychology in particular know that depression is a very complicated phenomenon indeed. It may have physical and genetic components. Body chemistry plays a role. Stress can be a causative factor. Sometimes depression can be a perfectly legitimate response to moral failure or to loss in one's life. Given the complexity of the phenomenon, a preacher who attempted to prescribe a "one size fits all" spiritual treatment for depression would in fact be in danger of doing great harm. People could walk away from such a sermon feeling very much worse instead of better. They might also make decisions that were not in their own best interests. The listeners would be better served if the preacher were to make general statements about how God wants to help people find healing and then to suggest that people battling depression get a medical checkup and consider therapy. In this sense, with preaching as with medicine, the first rule is "Do no harm."

Consider an additional example. Memorial Day and the Fourth of July are occasions in many churches for highly patriotic sermons that celebrate the virtues of the United States as a "Christian" nation. That claim itself is highly dubious historically, but in any case this year, in many churches, those usual assertions were tempered by the current political situation. As I write these lines in the summer of 2007, the country is bitterly divided over the present involvement in Iraq. People vehemently disagree over the legitimacy of the war, its necessity for national safety, and the timing and strategy of an American exit from the conflict. While the country remains united in support of and respect for the troops, serious questions have been raised about the right way to bring the conflict to an end.

Questions of right and wrong would seem to be perfect material for Christian sermons. Yet even here the preacher should be cautious. On the one hand, Christians are always for peace, always against violence, always ready to talk to enemies in the attempt to turn enemies into friends. On the other hand, in the calculus of international relations, knowing precisely which policies authentically serve the cause of peace is not always easy. A preacher who is not extremely well-read on the sources of the present conflict, the realities of Middle Eastern politics, historic Christian teachings regarding war, and the values of Islamic faith would be well advised to tread gently rather than make claims about what American policy should be.

So am I suggesting that timidity is a virtue in Christian preaching? No. But I am, in a slightly different context, commending Barth's suggestion of modesty. The media in recent years have been replete with egregious examples of clergy pronouncing "God's will" on every topic under the sun. Sometimes those pronouncements have been justified by clear biblical reasoning. More often, they have not. I believe that immodest impulse to moral dictation does great damage to the church in America in particular and the cause of Christ in general.

People do crave moral authority, and that is one of the things the church has to offer. But that authority is legitimate only when it is exercised in the context of thorough biblical exegesis, with careful examination of the facts of a given situation, earnest and selfless prayer, and a view to the larger witness of the church in the world. The Christian ethical principle of agape, to will and to work for the well-being of the other, comes into play in every situation to which the preacher attempts to speak. That principle can be served properly only when we preachers have done our homework. Going beyond the boundaries of your ability to study and comprehend a subject puts you in the category of Job, who "uttered what I did not understand, things too wonderful for me, which I did not know" (Job 42:3). As a result, the preacher who fails to understand and respect the complexities of moral discourse runs the risk of making herself and the church of Jesus look as though we don't know what we are talking about. We run the risk that people won't believe us when we do know what we are talking about—God's love for us through Jesus Christ.

A Modest Suggestion

Almost inevitably, any preacher who attempts to relate the gospel to present-day life sooner or later wants to speak from the pulpit concerning subjects in which he or she is not trained. All the cautions discussed above apply. But this also may be a time in which the usual procedure of a preacher's preparing her own message without assistance should be modified. Write out your sermon well in advance and then have one or two people who are expert in the field you are discussing read it, do a fact check for you, and give you feedback. If at all possible, get feedback from folks with differing perspectives on the issue. Your work will still be your own. You will still have to draw your own conclusions. But you won't be in the position of entering the pulpit with that nagging fear that you have missed something obvious. Once again, modesty in the assertions we make from the pulpit will serve us well.

CHAPTER 8

Render unto Caesar . . .

Preaching and Politics

Interim election, November 2006, the state of South Dakota. Petitions successfully force a statewide vote on a new
antiabortion law passed earlier by the state legislature.
The law would have forbidden virtually all abortions in
South Dakota, except where necessary to save the life of
the mother. Prochoice and prolife groups in the state, both
extremely religious, square off, each prepared to argue
that their position represents the will of God. Those on
the "Yes on 6" side, which is the prolife side, blanket the
state with blue-and-pink placards, many of them appear-
ing on the lawns of the state's churches. Prochoice pastors
preach prochoice sermons. Prolife pastors preach prolife
sermons. The law itself, and the question of whether it was
appropriately written to solve problems rather than caus-
ing more, tends to get lost in the rhetoric.

In this atmosphere, the Jones family went to church
that Sunday morning not really expecting to hear the sermon they heard. Their tradition trumpeted the idea of
separation of church and state. They themselves were very
conservative on the abortion issue but questioned whether
this was something that should be regulated by legislative
fiat. It seemed to them to be much more a personal moral
issue. But the pastor felt differently. He talked for half an

hour about the sanctity of life, working up to his climactic statement. "Now we're Baptists, and I can't tell you how to vote," he said. "But let me make one thing clear. Abortion is sin."

Sunday dinner at the Jones house was a troubled affair that day. "How could he say that?" Sally fumed. "Doesn't he know he's not supposed to tell people how to vote?"

"But he didn't," John answered. "In his mind, I think he was playing by the rules."

"Well, he pretty much said if you vote against this law, you're a sinner," Sally shot back. "Just because it's anti-abortion doesn't make it a good law."

"I know," John answered. "I wonder why he felt he had to preach on this subject anyway. He knows plenty of people in the church are on both sides of the issue. All this does is create conflict. Why didn't he just leave it alone?"

"I guess," Sally reflected, calming down, "that he thought this is the type of Christian moral issue where we have to be a witness in the public arena. But I've known too many women who've gone through this. I know these decisions are never easy. I wish Jesus had just told us clearly what to do!"

We will leave the Jones family there. Their story is fictional, but the facts of the South Dakota election in 2006 are not. Nor is the fact that the churches and the pulpits of South Dakota got heavily involved in that election. Nor is South Dakota's experience by any means unique. Throughout the history of the republic, preachers have sought to influence local, state, and national policy from their pulpits. On issues from alcohol to Sunday closing of liquor stores, from gambling to civil rights, from war to welfare, from tax exemption to school vouchers, the preachers of America have weighed in time and time again in the national debate. Sometimes preachers have successfully drawn a distinction between partisan politics and issues. J. Philip Wogaman, longtime professor of Christian ethics turned United Methodist pastor, draws what I believe to be the correct distinction. Preaching on issues is fine. Preaching partisan politics, advocating voting for one party or candidate over another, is not.[1] Sometimes preachers have confined their "political preaching" to instruction about what it means to be a good Christian citizen. More often though, I at least end up feeling that whenever the conservatives have been trying to affect national policy, liberal preachers have argued that the church should stay out of politics, and whenever the liberals have been trying to change national policy, conservative preachers have argued that the church should stay out of politics. Neither, in fact, has done so. All of which leaves us with the question for this chapter: what are the ethics of preaching about political issues?

The Legal Issue

In the United States, the doctrine of separation of church and state as enshrined in the First Amendment to the Constitution (although the phrase "separation of church and state" does not appear in the Constitution) has been taken to mean that Congress cannot tax or regulate religion and that religious institutions, in return, must not engage in partisan politics. On occasion, churches that have advocated partisan causes have had their tax-exempt status threatened or, in some cases, challenged. The distinction between acceptable preaching on issues and unacceptable partisan advocacy that Wogaman draws is usually considered to be the distinction between moral discourse with regard to an issue and actually supporting a particular candidate. The former is seen to be an appropriate function of the church. The latter is not. One quick answer to Sally's question above about whether the preacher should have preached as he did is that as long as he took a position on an issue and did not specifically advocate a candidate or a party platform, the preacher was playing within the rules.

Churches sometimes skate dangerously close to the legal precipice. The distribution of "voters' guides," which purport to be nonpartisan but in fact are not, in church narthexes or even passed out with the bulletins is not at all uncommon. Sometimes churches and pastors are even more blatant. The alliance of the past two decades between conservative evangelicals and the Republican Party has become a fact of the American political landscape. So has the assumption that the environment, civil rights, and other such causes are the property of the Christian left. Anomalies, such as the entry into the global-warming debate by evangelical pastor Rick Warren, are unusual enough to excite considerable comment. This leads us to the second issue for preachers and politics.

The Danger of Political Co-option

In the United States in 2007, the politicization of religion has led to a perception by many people that the church is little more than a voting bloc. Many people tend to assume that evangelicals vote Republican, that Catholics and mainline Protestants trend Democratic—that the more conservative one is theologically, the more likely one is support right-wing political causes. The danger both for those who preach and for those who listen is identifying the church of Jesus too closely with any one view of politics.

First, the idea that you can translate the teachings of Jesus directly into the political life of the nation smacks far too much of American hubris. It takes us back to that stream of Protestant preaching that attempts to identify the contemporary United States rather than biblical Israel as God's chosen nation. In so doing it ignores H. Richard Niebuhr's fundamental insight in *Christ and Culture*, that Christ stands over against and in criticism of every human culture and every nation's politics.[2] As William Willimon and Stanley Hauerwas point out, the church is a new community in every nation. "He [Christ] makes our fundamental categories, not 'Christ and Culture' (Richard Niebuhr), but 'Church and World' (Stanley Hauerwas)."[3] This alternative community does not make the church less interested in politics, but it does remind us that the church is of another, higher order that deserves our ultimate loyalties. And it keeps us from seeing any political party in any state as more than occasionally and serendipitously the party of God. Sometimes the Republicans in America get it right. Sometimes the Democrats do. Sometimes in Italy the Christian Democrats reflect Christian values better than the Socialists. Sometimes vice versa.

As the Christian ethicist John Bennett points out, the Scripture portrays the same Roman state as sometimes good and sometimes evil. "Two New Testament passages coming from different histori-cal situations reflect opposite attitudes toward the state: Romans 13:1-6 and Revelation 13. The former expressed Paul's hope that governing authorities [Rome] would be God's agent for good. The latter expressed the experience of Christians when persecuted by an evil state [Rome again!]."[4] Christians do not have the luxury of assuming that their party platform or their national policies reflect God's will in every situation.

Our second rule for preaching, then, after staying out of parti-san politics, is to remember that our "party" is Christ and Christ alone. The preacher as citizen may support whatever political par-ty she likes. The preacher as preacher works only for the cause of Jesus Christ. When that cause happens to intersect with a politi-cal issue, we may address it, but we dare not be seduced by the presumption that politics is the answer to the dilemmas of human life, or the church begins to look to the state for ultimate solutions, which is anathema to the gospel.

Deciding When to Preach Politics

What can happen to preachers caught up in dealing with issues is what happened in South Dakota in 2006. An issue comes along in the political arena that also engages Christian values, and the preacher is faced with the dilemma of whether to address it. With the cautions we have stated above, political preaching is permit-ted, but before we jump in, we must ask whether in a particular case it is wise.

That can be a difficult decision. Sometimes an issue is so hot, so divisive, that any attention from the pulpit would only ignite further controversy. Sometimes, as in the civil rights struggle in the South, the gospel runs so contrary to public opinion that the preacher must decide whether the risks to life, limb, family, and job are worth it. Sometimes an issue is too new, too unformed, and attempting to stake out an ethical position from the pulpit would be premature. Some issues are simply better dealt with in formats other than proclamation. Sometimes the larger agenda of the church is so focused in other directions that the preacher may decide that dealing with a particular issue presents an unacceptable distraction from the church's mission.

The preacher needs to ask himself questions like: Is there a clear biblical word with regard to this issue? Will dealing with this issue from the pulpit help members of the congregation in their Christian growth? Can I be fair to both sides?[5] What would be the consequences of not preaching on this issue? Is this a transient tempest, or is there an enduring Christian value at stake here? Must I do this as a matter of faithfulness to Christ? Not every political subject rises to the level of a faith issue. Only when the preacher is convinced that she has something important to say, that more good than harm can be done by saying it, and that people will both be able to hear and to learn from her approach should she move forward to the next step in the process.

Preaching a "Political" Sermon

In chapter 7, I borrowed and adapted Karl Barth's idea of modesty in approaching scriptural interpretation. I suggested that the preacher should be modest in making factual assertions. Modesty seems to me to be essential in political preaching as well. Seldom does the republic stand or fall on the basis of what we preach. Even the Rev. Dr. Martin Luther King Jr., preaching about the bus boycott in the Dexter Avenue Baptist Church in Montgomery in 1955, could not know the impact his preaching would have. His work helped spark a movement that did change the republic. But as the events themselves demonstrated, that movement was more about the purposes of God than it was about any one preacher.

So it is best for the preacher to approach a political subject with a limited goal. Usually that goal will be to help the congregation understand the issue from a biblical, Christian, church point of view. As she writes her sermon, the preacher should keep that goal of understanding in mind. Take, for example, the national situation in the late summer of 2007 with regard to the war in Iraq. On the one hand, national polls suggest that the great majority of the population has turned against the war and wants our troops to come home as soon as possible. On the other hand, a substantial minority, mostly in the president's political party, continues to view the war as necessary for national security. In many churches, preachers have limited themselves to praying for peace and for the safety of the troops. But what if a preacher decides he or she needs to address the situation from a Christian point of view? What goal could such a sermon have?

For many preachers, attempting to limit the goal for a sermon on a topic such as this would be frustrating. What many of us want to do when we preach political sermons is thunder righteousness. Often we would like to talk constitutional theory or offer civics lessons. But while those things may be a badly needed part of the national conversation, they are not the purpose of a Christian sermon. The purpose of a Christian sermon must always include upholding the teachings of Christ, particularly, and the values taught in Scripture, generally, at the same time that we help the congregation understand how those values apply. Note the difference. Certain Old Testament teachings on holy war and the appropriate techniques of combat stand in stark contrast to Jesus's "Blessed are the peacemakers" (Matt. 5:9). And Jesus himself said, "I have not come to bring peace, but a sword" (Matt. 10:34).

So the goal of a sermon referring to the war in Iraq might be to help the congregation understand Christian teachings on peace. What does the Bible really say about making war and making peace, and how have those teachings been interpreted in Christian history? The preacher who wishes to critique specific government policies may do so only in a nonpartisan way and with reference to how those policies do or do not cohere with biblical values.

But what if I just want to preach against (or for) the war and say how the government's prosecution of the war is not (or is) the right thing to do? Christian preachers throughout history have seen it as their duty on occasion to speak truth to power. The question is, what truth? A Christian preacher's primary subject matter is the witness of Scripture to the purposes of God in the world. When a nation's policies conflict with the purposes of God, we have both a right and a duty to say so. On the other hand, when you take a specific partisan position on a partisan issue, no matter what that issue might be, you run the very real risk of leaving the realm of Christian preaching and entering the realm of political discourse.

You risk losing sight of that Christ who is above all circumstances and all nations. You may choose to go forward anyway, but if you do, it is important to realize precisely what you in fact are doing.

Let's say, though, that you have chosen a limited, nonpartisan goal for your political sermon, and you are ready to move forward to the next step in preparation. The next steps are little different from the preparation a responsible pastor does for any sermon. Double-check your interpretation of Scripture. Gather as much information as you can from reliable sources on both sides of the issue. Be sure that you understand precisely how this issue is being worked out in the realm of public policy. With regard to the South Dakota election battle in 2006, for example, many people who were themselves basically against abortion as a discretionary means of birth control ended up voting against the statute as it was written. They felt the language of the statute failed to leave enough room for the decisions of a woman and her doctor. That kind of distinction, however, would be very difficult to draw in a sermon on the issue. The point here is not to discuss that particular controversy. It is to say that the preacher must always keep in mind that fine line between a Christian value as defined in Scripture and the way that value is or is not translated into workable public policy.

When you are clear about the applicable biblical values and the details of the political issue as it is currently being discussed, then you are ready to begin crafting a sermon. Keeping in mind as you write the particular needs of your own congregation is essential, of course. If the issue is partisan, very few congregations will not have people on both sides. That means the tone of the sermon must be respectful toward differing opinions. In his book on preaching on controversial issues, Adam Hamilton advocates structuring a controversial sermon so that before you take a position, you do your best to present fairly the arguments of both sides. I will explore this in some detail in chapter 10. When you hold a strong opinion yourself, this may be very difficult to do. But it represents an essential pastoral step in this kind of preaching. People with whom you disagree will be much more likely to listen with an open mind if they know that you have understood and appreciated their perspective on the issue. People with whom you agree will have friends and family who disagree. They will need to know that those they love have been treated gently. Again, we come back to Barth's theme of modesty. Much of the damage that is done in political preaching is not so much in the positions that are taken as in the tone in which those sermons are couched and presented.

The final step in crafting a sermon on a political issue is then to take a position, to explain what that position is, and to say why you advocate it. Remember that for this political sermon to be a Christian sermon, the preacher must ruthlessly eliminate any arguments that derive from partisan or personal considerations. You are attempting to bring biblical truth to a political issue, nothing more and nothing less. Here again, the tone of what you say is crucial. Gentleness and modesty are the order of the day. Communicating anger will only tend to alienate those with whom you disagree and consequently to polarize the congregation.

Some, on reading this chapter, may say that I have placed so many strictures on political preaching as to make it hardly worth doing at all. My intent is to suggest that, more than almost any other preaching we might choose to do, this area is fraught with both practical and theological danger. Preaching about political issues is dangerous practically because it often alienates those we are attempting to reach and educate in the faith. It is dangerous theologically because it runs the risk of making proximate issues in a given society appear to be ultimate, which is idolatry. Some of my caution, of course, comes from my Baptist background with its emphasis on the necessity of the separation of church and state. The Lutheran tradition, similarly, tends to see the church and the state as separate entities with distinct purposes. Also true is that I have a personal pastoral conviction that political preaching, while not necessarily unethical, can often be essentially counter-productive and therefore unwise. And it is further true that I have witnessed the political preaching of television preachers and popular demagogues who seem to me to have shamefully abused the gospel for the sake of their own political agendas. These convictions have informed both my caution in endorsing political preaching and the strictures I have suggested in crafting a political sermon.

All cautions aside, however, one more thing needs to be said. God does from time to time call a Martin Luther King Jr. or an

Oscar Romero or a Dietrich Bonhoeffer or a Desmond Tutu to preach gospel truths that are at the same time clearly and powerfully political. When that happens the world is changed. The key things to remember are (1) that the timing for those moments when gospel and politics intersect is God's and not ours and (2) that very often those who are called to preach God's politics in these *kairos* moments pay a very heavy price indeed.

After the Sermon

More than any other preaching we may do, with the exception of general preaching on controversial issues (chapter 10), political preaching requires careful consideration of managing what happens in the congregation after the sermon is preached. When they are dealing with issues, people require time to process what has been said.

Sometimes a preacher will preach a political sermon and then invite comments and feedback from the congregation as part of the service itself. At other times he or she may encourage the congregation to meet at a later time to discuss what has been said. If the preacher presents the sermon as an invitation to dialogue, people will feel freer to ask questions, disagree, and work out their own answers to the issue. Such conversations can help teach a congregation how to disagree agreeably and perhaps how to move toward consensus on issues.

The ubiquity of the Internet presents additional opportunities for sermon follow-up. The preacher might, for example, post the manuscript of a sermon as a blog and encourage people to respond to what has been written in a threaded discussion format. This format both gives people time to think about their response and allows them to reply in writing. Some people are much better at expressing themselves clearly in written format than they would be in a face-to-face discussion.

Also, when doing this kind of preaching, recruit a group of people in the congregation to serve as designated listeners. Such a group could be useful in several ways. They could respond publicly to the sermon, either immediately or later, giving their own points of agreement and disagreement as church members. They could act as verbal mirrors for the preacher, telling him or her what they have heard the sermon say. In this way, the preacher learns whether he or she has successfully communicated what was intended. They could solicit feedback from other members of the congregation to provide wider data on what was heard and how the people responded to it. They will inevitably act as interpreters, helping the congregation clarify their understanding of what has been said. Very often their help can prevent an initial misperception from snowballing into something more extensive and serious.

It is also important that the preacher pay attention to whatever pastoral issues might arise as a result of political preaching. Say, for example, that a preacher decides to preach a sermon either for or against the imprisonment of suspected terrorists without the protections available to citizens of the United States. Any number of people in the congregation may hear such a sermon through the filter of their own experience. Many congregations these days include family members of those serving in the military or as civilian contractors in Iraq. Some may have family members or friends who have died or been injured there or in past military conflicts. Others may themselves be serving in the military or the National Guard and anticipate the possibility of deployment. Veterans of World War II, Korea, Vietnam, and Desert Storm might hear such a sermon in the light of their own experiences and understandings. I once pastored a congregation that included a leading and rather controversial and opinionated member of Congress. After a political sermon, any or all of these folks might well require special pastoral attention as they think about what they have heard.

For some in the congregation, the consequence of a political sermon will be a change in their relationship with their pastor. People who have always assumed that they and their pastor were in agreement on a given issue may discover that they do not agree at all. Some will take such a disagreement in stride, realizing that no two people in this life ever agree about everything unless one of them has no brain. Others may find it exceedingly difficult to continue to trust the pastor while disagreeing. Anyone who has been a pastor for very long knows that people are perfectly capable of getting upset and leaving a congregation over the silliest of issues or no issue at all. If we allow ourselves to worry about how people might react to what we say, that worry could keep us from ever saying anything at all. Jesus himself seemed to be much more interested in telling people the truth than he was in not hurting their feelings. Still, it is well to remember that politics is a particularly intense and volatile subject for many people. The preacher who mixes politics and religion is virtually guaranteed to upset significant numbers of people in the process. That reality bids us consider carefully both before and after we choose to speak. A pastor's primary job is to help people interpret life in terms of the gospel. To the degree that a political sermon helps people understand an issue from the perspective of the faith, we can preach it, as long as we do so carefully.

CHAPTER 9

Care for the Flock in Your Charge

Preaching in Times of Crisis

It was just after 8:30 in the morning on Tuesday, September 11, 2001. Pastor Ron was at his desk, getting ready for the morning staff meeting when his phone rang with the first call of the day. It was his wife, Sheryl, with the news of the first plane hitting the World Trade Center. And that, of course, was the last moment of normalcy for days to come.

At first the staff tried to go on with their routine. After all, signals needed to be checked, the week's work lined out, a service planned. Church programs were revving up for the fall. Denial is often our first reaction to crisis. And New York is a long way from Louisville. But then a few minutes later the second plane hit the second tower. The news of the Pentagon attack came through. And everybody realized this was no accident. Anxiously they gathered around a portable TV in the church office. Together they watched horrified as the towers fell, heard the story of the crash in Pennsylvania. By noon the church was open for the first of many prayer services that week. Church folk and members of the public were calling and stopping by with prayer concerns for family out of touch in New York and Washington, D.C., or simply trapped somewhere by the grounding of all U.S. flights.

By Thursday morning, the day he routinely prepared his sermons, Ron had long since realized that his plans for the week were out the window. A grim mood of national crisis had settled in. Hope for survivors in the rubble was beginning to fade. And people would be coming to church that Sunday desperate for a word from the Lord. It was his job to provide it! But what? And how? He had never felt more inadequate. So he set to work, and this is what he came up with.

Going Forward
Psalm 64; Matthew 5:38-48
Sunday after the Attack, September 16, 2001
Ron Sisk Preaching

So how do the people of God respond when evil takes form and shape and rains down terror in our midst? We are only just beginning to find our way. We are shocked. We are angry. We grieve. We are more than a little bit afraid. It is not too much to say we are forever changed. If I had words that would take all the pain away this morning, I would offer them gladly, but there is no panacea. Like December 7, 1941, September 11, 2001, is a day that will live in infamy. And you and I must somehow find a way forward in this new reality. So this morning, as a beginning, I want offer three simple thoughts inspired by the Scripture.

First, God is our refuge. One of the first things people always ask when heinous evil erupts is, "Where was God in all this?" "How could God let this happen?" There are two answers. From a systematic-theology perspective, the answer is that God's greatest gift to humankind is the gift of freedom. God has made us able to choose. But that very gift carries within itself the possibility that we will choose hate instead of love, evil instead of good. And that is what happened Tuesday morning. Just as God's own angel Lucifer, Son of the Morning, did before them, so nineteen of God's own creatures [the terrorists] chose evil and fell from the heavens into hell. As long as God leaves us free, you and I will live with the possibility of evil.

But there is another answer to the question, where was God this Tuesday morning? And that is the answer the Son of God gave us with his body and his blood so long ago. Just as Jesus came to show us that God's love is here for you and me, so also I believe, Christ was there. Christ was there with the hijack victims on those planes, the pilots and flight attendants and passengers. Christ was there with the office workers caught up in sudden panic. Christ was there as they struggled to help one another down the stairs. Christ was there with the firefighters and the EMS workers and the police. Christ fell with them as those buildings fell. Christ is there this morning in the dust and the rubble as hope for survivors is fading. Whether they name his name or know to call on him or not, Christ is there with the families who grieve. When you and I suffer, Christ suffers with us. That's what that cross is all about.

Second, though, evil will not win. Evil cannot hide. The truth will out. And judgment is certain. As the investigations have gone on this week, it has become more and more clear that the perpetrators of these attacks were Middle Eastern terrorists, most likely the servants of Osama bin Laden. The organizations that recruited and trained and supported them must be found, and they must be stopped. During the early days of World War II, there were many Christians who believed we should not retaliate against the Nazis, that the only Christian thing to do is always to seek reconciliation. In the face of that argument the theologian Reinhold Niebuhr said a clear and resounding No. There is such a thing as a just war, Niebuhr said. Sometimes reconciliation is not possible. Sometimes evil threatens the very survival of freedom itself. And when it does, that evil must be resisted. So long as it is fought by just means, the war on terrorism is a just war. Having said that, though . . .

There is a third thought we must reach out toward this day and in the days ahead. And that is that Christ calls us toward a better way. Glen Stassen, whom many of us know and who was a member of this congregation for many years, has written extensively on Christ's teachings about peace. Stassen says what Christ has given us here in the Sermon on the Mount is a pattern for Christian action he calls the "transforming initiative." The idea is simply this. Whenever we are at odds with anyone, your job and mine as Christians is to look for the root of that conflict, and if we can identify the root of the conflict, look for what we can do to make things better. Going the second mile is a transforming initiative. Praying for your enemies is a transforming initiative. Seeking to understand is a transforming initiative. From a national political standpoint, one transforming initiative in this situation would be to press [Yasir] Arafat and [Ariel] Sharon for a truly evenhanded and just solution to the Palestinian question. And here at home, if you have an Arab or Islamic coworker or friend or neighbor, one thing you might do this afternoon is give them a call and say to them that you know this is not what Islam is all about. Listen as they tell you how difficult this week has been for them. Let them know that you know it's not their fault.

The last verse in Matthew 5 is that one we normally translate "Be perfect . . . as your heavenly Father is perfect." The Greek word we translate as "perfect" really means "be mature" or even "be wise." If ever there was a time in America when we needed maturity, my sisters and brothers, this is that time. So let us as Christian people transform our talking and our doing in these days with the Spirit of Christ. Let us remember that hatred only puts us on the same level as our enemies. Let us use what force we must, but let us not be fooled into putting our trust in force. [Fyodor] Dostoyevsky writes, "At some ideas you stand perplexed, especially at the sight of human sins, uncertain whether to combat it by force or by humble love. Always decide, 'I will combat it with humble love.' If you make up your mind about that once and for all, you can conquer the whole world."[1] The last time so many people died by violence on American soil was a hundred and forty years ago, during the American Civil War. As that war was ending, President Abraham Lincoln was inaugurated a second time. The last paragraph of his speech then, I think, suggests the spirit of how you and I can go forward in the days ahead:

> With malice toward none, with charity for all, with firmness in the right as God gives us to see the right, let us strive on to finish the work we are in, to bind up the nation's wounds, to care for [the one] who shall have borne the battle and for [the] widow and [the] orphan, to do all which may achieve and cherish a just and lasting peace among ourselves and with all nations.[2]

Thus let it be always with us.

I include this story of my experience of 9/11 and the sermon I preached on the following Sunday not necessarily as an example of how it ought to be done, but rather as a touch point for discussion as we consider the ethics of preaching in crisis.[3] In my twenty years as a pastor, not many Sundays like September 16, 2001, had come along. But come they did. Some crises were national in scale, such as the first Sunday of the first Gulf War of 1990-91. Some crises were regional. My wife and I happened to be living in the San Francisco Bay Area in 1989 during the earthquake that collapsed the Bay Bridge and devastated sections of the city. Some crises were local, such as accidental deaths or fires or storms. Some crises wouldn't have been considered crises at all by anyone outside a fairly narrow circle. The Baptist denomination I was part of in those years was in the midst of a virulent controversy that occasionally spilled over into the local church. One could argue, I suppose, that this chapter would be more appropriate in a book about pastoral care than in one about homiletical ethics. Still, there are ways to preach in a crisis and ways not to preach in a crisis, and discussion about how to preach crisis sermons seems to me to be appropriate in a book on preaching ethically.

Preliminary Considerations

The first thing to remember in a crisis is that people will be very upset. They will be listening far more from the rhetorical pole of *pathos* than from that of *logos*. The Sunday after the tornado hits town is not the time for the preacher to offer restrained, rational analysis of the weather patterns that cause tornadoes in the Midwest. It is the time to help the congregation members identify the emotions they are feeling. Shock, anger, fear, and a dozen other feelings will be vying for expression. Whatever else we do, we who preach need to help people identify and validate all those tumultuous feelings as a matter of pastoral care. Sometimes people need to be reminded that it is OK to feel even feelings that they don't understand or that frighten them. Note that the introduction to my sermon above is focused on the emotional responses to the attack. And then we need to give them some positive way to begin dealing with this new reality the crisis has created. Crisis sermons should be unashamedly pastoral.

Second, with regard to the whole worship service, the Sunday after a crisis is not the time to get creative. People need the comfort of the familiar when crises come. They need a relatively familiar liturgy. This is not the time to teach them a new hymn or the latest chorus. This is the time for music that transcends generations and worship styles, that falls within what the musicians call the "hymnic memory" of the vast majority of folks. That is why at the televised national services after 9/11 you heard hymns like "A Mighty Fortress Is Our God" sung over and over again. Whatever comfort means in your context, that is what you should do.

Third, if praying even more than you ordinarily do in preparation for a sermon is possible, this is the week to do that. We hope, of course, that the Spirit speaks through us every time we preach. Many people reading this chapter know that their lives as preachers are organized every week of the year around the discipline of prayer. But in crisis times we preach out of that anguish in which our souls cry out to God for answers. We preach to people who are themselves crying out for answers too. It is out of our common plea to God far more than out of any homiletical excellence that answers will begin to come both for those of us who speak and for those who listen.

Choosing the Text

A strong text is essential for a crisis sermon. That text should focus on grand themes of the faith such as comfort, assurance, providence, and the like. In times like these, people need to be reminded as strongly as possible that God is with all of us in every moment of our lives, whether we feel God's presence or not.

For many of us, certain texts leap to mind when we think of comfort, texts such as Jeremiah 29:11, "For surely I know the plans I have for you, says the LORD, plans for your welfare and not for harm, to give you a future with hope." A crisis Sunday may therefore be a day when we choose a text that will add the comfort of familiarity to the inherent strength of its reassurance. On the Sunday after the San Francisco earthquake, I chose to preach from one of the favorite psalms of my childhood, Psalm 121. That psalm begins with the familiar line, "I lift up my eyes to the hills—from where will my help come?" I chose the psalm for its reassurance, not really thinking at all about its first line. But in subsequent study as I was preparing to write, I discovered that the psalm was meant to be sung as pilgrims were going up to Jerusalem to worship. That meant the hills weren't the source of the help. They were the source of danger from robbers and brigands along the way. The pilgrims weren't watching the hills for reassurance; they were scanning them for signs of danger. In an area where earthquakes commonly lead to landslides from the unstable hills, the psalm suddenly took on a more vivid meaning than I had anticipated. Choosing a text for its reassurance is perhaps the most common way preachers deal with the demands of a crisis Sunday. But sometimes that text will offer up more than we hope.

Choosing a text for reassurance in a crisis is also the most ethical choice in that it demonstrates faithfulness to the pastoral calling to serve the needs of the congregation, but it is not always the choice that preachers make. In the aftermath of the devastation of New Orleans by Hurricane Katrina in 2005, for example, one prominent preacher chose to use the event as an opportunity to castigate the people of New Orleans for their sinfulness and to portray the hurricane as the judgment of God on New Orleans vice. At least three things were wrong with that kind of sermon. First of all, the declaration of the judgment of God is not ours to make. Such a pronouncement belongs to the One who makes the decision. Second, the preacher did not tell the full story. Had the preacher talked about the foolishness of local, state, and national authorities in flood prevention and emergency planning for New Orleans and the sense that God's judgment consists in part in allowing us to experience the consequences of our actions, he might have had a point. But, third, that would not have been, in any case, the Sunday to talk about judgment!

As a related comment, let me point out that, in my opinion, the most serious error I made in my own sermon after 9/11 was the error of consigning the nineteen conspirators to hell. That amounted on my part to a presumption of the prerogatives of God. No preacher is authorized to pronounce judgment. Judgment is for God alone.

In many traditions, the texts for sermons are normally chosen from the lectionary. Some weeks before September 11, I had decided that on September 16 I would preach out of the lectionary texts for that day. After the attack, I chose to change the texts to reflect the suddenness and conspiracy of the attack and the Christian ideal in dealing with enemies. I chose Psalm 64 and Mathew 5:38-48.

> Hear my voice, O God, in my complaint;
>   preserve my life from the dread enemy.
> Hide me from the secret plots of the wicked,
>   from the scheming of evildoers,
> who whet their tongues like swords,
>   who aim bitter words like arrows,
> shooting from ambush at the blameless;
>   they shoot suddenly and without fear.
> They hold fast to their evil purpose;
>   they talk of laying snares secretly,

thinking, "Who can see us?
    Who can search out our crimes?
We have thought out a cunningly conceived plot."
    For the human heart and mind are deep.
But God will shoot his arrow at them;
    they will be wounded suddenly.
Because of their tongue he will bring them to ruin;
    all who see them will shake with horror.
Then everyone will fear;
    they will tell what God has brought about,
    and ponder what he has done.
Let the righteous rejoice in the LORD
    and take refuge in him.
Let all the upright in heart glory.
—Psalm 64

[Jesus said,] "You have heard that it was said, 'An eye for an eye and a tooth for a tooth.' But I say to you, Do not resist an evil-doer. But if anyone strikes you on the right cheek, turn the other also; and if anyone wants to sue you and take your coat, give your cloak as well; and if anyone forces you to go one mile, go also the second mile. Give to everyone who begs from you, and do not refuse anyone who wants to borrow from you.

"You have heard that it was said, 'You shall love your neighbor and hate your enemy.' But I say to you, Love your enemies and pray for those who persecute you, so that you may be children of your Father in heaven; for he makes his sun rise on the evil and on the good, and sends rain on the righteous and on the unrighteous. For if you love those who love you, what reward do you have? Do not even the tax collectors do the same? And if you greet only your brothers and sisters, what more are you doing than others? Do not even the Gentiles do the same? Be perfect, therefore, as your heavenly Father is perfect.
—Matthew 5:38-48

No doubt other preachers chose quite differently. Many may have chosen to go on with the lectionary texts for the day and

find the word of the Lord from within those texts. That is a legitimate choice that has the virtue of uniting the congregation with
the broader church as one preaches.

I was hearing so much anger, though, and I was so angry myself,[4] that I wanted to attempt to move us beyond that initial anger
toward a more thoughtful response to the attack. My own sense
was that people needed to be reminded both that God does see
and judge all human actions and that Christians are responsible
for how we respond even to unprovoked and sudden attack. In the
midst of the heat of the moment, I wanted to point to the Christian
ideal. This was the reasoning behind the texts I chose.

Crafting the Sermon

As noted above, I believe it is important to begin with an acknowledgment of the feelings of the congregation, no matter what the
crisis might be. Sometimes those feelings may be clear and strong,
as they were for so many of us after September 11. At other times
they may be confused and confusing. Crises may be dramatic, but
they—and our responses—are not necessarily simple. It is important, though, that the preacher on such a day make an attempt
early on to identify and validate the feelings inherent in people's
responses to what has happened.

Notice that I chose to address two of the big theological questions people ask. I did this because the church I served at the time
was well educated and used to theological discourse. They really
wanted to know how God could let such a thing happen, and they
wanted to know where God was while it was happening. In fact,
those were the questions I had been getting from people in one
way or another every day that week. In a sense, giving adequate
answers is not even as important as acknowledging the questions.
I couldn't hope to answer such global questions adequately, and
many times preachers who come after me won't be able to do so
either. Sometimes the common struggle toward faith is the very
best thing we can say.

It is important also, though, that we not delve into such questions too deeply in a crisis sermon. When feelings run so high, peo-

ple aren't capable of listening to complicated theological discourse. In my tradition, a typical Sunday morning sermon runs twenty to twenty-five minutes. In crisis times I would usually abbreviate that time frame by about a third, as I did with the example above. A couple of simple points that people can hold onto and take with them will do the best job of providing comfort on such a day.

After addressing people's feelings and their questions, put the event in the context of faith in a way that looks forward. As I sought to do this for our congregation that September, I found myself having to deal with my own ethical position with regard to war. I believe that it is possible for Christians to be forced to war as a last resort to resist aggressive evil. I hold that position in harmony with classical Christian just war theory as I understand it. But I also recognize that that position is an essentially pragmatic ethic that falls short of the peacemaking ideal laid out by Christ himself. I knew that the congregation would hold opinions spread all across the spectrum regarding how best to respond to the attack.

I chose both to be faithful to my own sense that the terrorist attack constituted an evil that must be resisted and to remind the congregation that Christians seek a better way. As I did so, I trusted that what I saw as a personally necessary nuancing of my position would also serve the conflicted feelings many in the congregation had to be experiencing.

My struggle that week serves as a reminder that ethical preaching during a crisis must often be done "on the fly" in the midst of a developing situation. You don't have a lot of time to develop your theology of natural evil when the tornado comes through on Thursday night and you have to stand in front of battered townsfolk on Sunday morning. As much as is possible on a morning such as that, it is best to restrict your assertions to the essentials of the faith upon which all Christians agree.

The final element that I included in my crisis sermon that morning was to begin to point the congregation members toward practical things they could do. People in crisis situations often feel helpless and at a loss as to what to do next. Sometimes, if the crisis is at home, they will need encouragement to take hold and get on about the business of recovery. In our situation in Louisville that week, we were removed geographically from the locations of greatest need. Collections had begun, and a few people were driving to New York to work at Ground Zero, but beyond praying with and comforting those still waiting for word about friends and loved ones, there wasn't much we could actually do. I was especially concerned in those days that people were generalizing their anger toward the terrorists and misdirecting it toward all Muslims. We had a sizeable Muslim population in our town. We even had one Muslim who worshiped regularly in our church. So I suggested that folk reach out to those Muslims they knew.

I then closed the sermon by suggesting an attitude based on Christ's teachings about peacemaking with which we could move forward. Out of that attitude I hoped the congregation could begin to find ways to address some of the root causes that might lead to such an attack.

Crises differ widely. The preacher is in a very different place dealing with terrorist attack than she is dealing with storm or flood or fire or accident. But my own experience tends to suggest that certain key elements—validating feelings, answering questions, pointing to the faith, and suggesting practical steps forward—can be used in most crisis sermons.

Final Cautions

I have a few remaining general cautions to help keep a crisis sermon from becoming something it ought not to be. First, it is essential not to use a crisis sermon as an excuse to pursue some other agenda we may have with the congregation. Everybody's emotions, including our own, are raw during a crisis. If we have unfinished agendas or unresolved emotional issues with the congregation, a crisis sermon could be a time when those issues find their way to the surface: "If you'd listened to me when I tried to get you to build a storm shelter . . ." Deal with crises on their own, rather than lumping them with whatever other issues you might have. Even if you are sure the crisis is the church's own fault, this is not the time to say that.

Second, in a crisis sermon be very careful about assigning blame to anyone. That Sunday after 9/11 we were beginning to hear that Osama bin Laden was the source of the plot, but nobody was certain. I can remember debating whether to mention his name. I chose to go ahead because the best news sources I could get were beginning to suggest relative certainty. Very often allowing some time to pass before we attempt to assign responsibility for an event or refraining from assigning responsibility at all is the better part of wisdom. This is especially important in more local crises, when we are dealing with grief situations such as death in traffic accidents. Often people want to go straight to questions such as "Were they drinking?" or "Were they wearing their seatbelts?" I can understand the impulse to try to keep others from making mistakes, but I believe dwelling on such things during the crisis itself simply serves to worsen the anguish the family is already feeling. The pastoral realities of death and loss should be our focus. Others can address contributing factors as time goes on.

Third, when the crisis is a result of natural evil, such as a flood or a tornado, some people will want to move straight to talk of the will of God. Was it God's will, for example, that people die as a result of the San Francisco earthquake in 1989? No, of course not. We chose to build a city on the San Andreas fault line and to continue living in that earthquake zone, knowing that such events would happen from time to time. The deaths were tragic realities of the human condition. Miracles do happen, but we can't expect God, in the normal course of things, to alter the processes of nature on our behalf. It is also important here that we refrain from suggesting from the pulpit that God alters nature to protect one person or family when that alteration brings injury to someone else. You often hear statements such as, "God protected the Jones family farm on Saturday. God sent that tornado to Goodletsville instead." We forget that the folks in Goodletsville might well have something to say about that!

Fourth, regardless of how brilliant our crisis preaching may be, we should remember that very often in a crisis time, people will be able to hear and absorb very little of what we have to say. Often so much is going on in their own minds and emotions that our carefully argued comforts come across as so much noise. Restraint becomes a key value in preaching at such times. These are the times to show by our presence and by our actions that we care. In the week after 9/11 our church, like many congregations across the country, held several prayer services, almost always without sermons. People came and drew comfort from being together. Sometimes we preach best in crises by providing people other things besides sermons—a hug, a listening ear, or a heartfelt prayer.

Done well, crisis preaching can capture the anguish and unite the souls of a people in the midst of terrible times. As I was writing this chapter, the Interstate 35 bridge collapsed in Minneapolis, killing some and injuring dozens. My prayer is that the preachers of that city and all who read this book and serve the people of God will comfort their people well when crisis comes. Such preaching, in addition to being pastorally appropriate, represents an ethical choice to serve the needs of your congregation.

CHAPTER 10

Your Neighbor as Yourself

Preaching on Controversial Issues

Beth knew by the time the recessional began that she had done something terribly wrong. She had known, of course, that the death penalty was a controversial topic at St. Luke's. She had read the statistic that two-thirds of the American public continued to favor the death penalty despite church opposition, its failure as a deterrent, and recent cases proving a number of false convictions. But she had thought the folks at St. Luke's would be ready to hear her perspective.

The truth is Beth loved St. Luke's. She had been their pastor for only two years. She still felt that thrill of joy every morning as she drove into the parking lot and looked at the white clapboard New England–style building with its nineteenth-century stained glass. And she had found the people to be warm, welcoming, and gracious; a typical small-town mix of teachers, business people, and farmers. If anything, they were probably better educated than a lot of congregations, with three doctors and two professors from the nearby college in the church.

She had thought they would be ready to hear her views. She had even picked the commandment "Thou shalt not kill" as her Old Testament text, pairing it with Jesus's words about anger in the Sermon on the Mount. And she had chosen the upcoming execution at the state prison as a moment when people would be thinking about the issue anyway. She had built her arguments carefully, laying out in detail why she believed capital punishment to be a denial of the Christian witness.

Beth was sensitive to atmosphere, though. And the more she had talked, the more she had realized the congregation wasn't with her at all. They had stopped looking up. One or two had turned red in the face. A few were whispering to one another. Now, with the service ending, the room felt colder and more uncomfortable, more hostile than she had ever experienced it.

"Lord," she prayed as she walked toward the door to greet the worshipers on their way out, "what did I do? What did I say? How will I ever fix this?"

Maybe it isn't as bad as Beth thinks it is. We will let her figure that out. If she is a Baptist, her deacons will probably tell her exactly how the sermon was received. Her dilemma, though, takes us to one of the most difficult issues in preaching. How do you preach ethically on controversial issues? More than any other chapter of this book, this one covers ground that others have already plowed. The homiletics literature includes books such as the United Methodist pastor Adam Hamilton's *Confronting the Controversies: A Christian Looks at the Tough Issues*,[1] his colleague Philip Wogaman's *Speaking the Truth in Love: Prophetic Preaching to a Broken World*,[2] and Christine Smith's *Preaching as Weeping, Confession, and Resistance: Radical Responses to Radical Evil*.[3] One of my favorites of the genre, for its title alone, is Tony Campolo's *Is Jesus a Republican or a Democrat? And 14 Other Polarizing Issues*.[4] Sometimes these works consist of sermons themselves. Others are a mixture of sermons and suggestions of approaches to the task of preaching on controversial topics. In these works and others on preaching on controversial issues, I see two broad approaches that represent the range of thought on this matter. They fall loosely into the traditional tension between preaching prophetically and preaching pastorally.

Prophetic Preaching on Controversial Issues

In this context, *prophetic* preaching may be taken to mean advocating the interests of a particular minority or oppressed group over against the insensitivity or self-interest of the majority. Its purpose is to raise the consciousness of the church, to make people intensely and often uncomfortably aware of issues.

Prophetic preaching has a long and honored history in America, particularly in the work of civil rights and peacemaking. From the colonial period forward, abolitionists fought the institution of slavery from the pulpit. The Rev. Dr. Martin Luther King Jr. and the civil rights preachers of the 1950s and 1960s stand solidly within that prophetic tradition. Much of the antiwar movement of the 1960s and 1970s also found impetus in the pulpits of prophets such as William Sloane Coffin, especially during his tenure as pastor of Riverside Church in New York City.

Prophetic preaching on controversial issues tends to be fairly simple in structure. It defines an issue, cites a governing biblical text, and develops an argument out of that text. Christine Smith's and Tony Campolo's books cited above are examples of this type of approach to preaching, one from a mainline and the other from an evangelical point of view.

In Smith's book, she defines and opposes a series of what she terms "radical evils." "Preaching," she argues, "is . . . an act of naming. The naming of reality functions in many ways, but whether naming calls persons to claim the fullness of their own created worth and the worth of all creation, or whether naming enables the demonic powers of hatred and injustice to be exposed and dethroned, one can hardly dispute the power of publicly proclaimed words."[5] Smith's first chapter, for example, names the evil of "handicappism," states how the church should confront the marginalization of those with disabilities in church and society, and makes suggestions for appropriate theological concepts to use in preaching such sermons. She points to "And the Word became flesh and lived among us, . . . full of grace and truth" (John 1:14) as an opportunity to rethink what it means to be flesh, especially for one who cannot hear or see or understand as others do.[6] Her controlling metaphor of preaching as weeping, confession, and resistance suggests that it is the preacher's job to make the church aware of various forms of oppression and to move people toward resistance to those oppressions.

Campolo approaches prophetic preaching from the standpoint of an evangelical preacher who views himself as somewhat out of step with many evangelicals on a number of controversial issues. His chapters are essentially reflective essays that offer his perspectives on various issues. I have heard him use much of the material from this book in sermons. While he attempts to present both sides of an argument, his approach is to point out the flaws in the side he disagrees with on the way to arguing for his own position on an issue. Since these are not precisely sermons, he does not necessarily use a governing text, though he sprinkles scripture passages throughout his essays.

In many ways, the kind of prophetic preaching done by Campolo, Smith, and many others is typical of preaching on controversial issues. It consists of reasoned argument designed to convince the hearer that the preacher's perspective is correct biblically and theologically. This preaching is an ancient and honorable tradition among biblical people. Many of us can identify issues about which, with Tevye in *Fiddler on the Roof*, we would like to declare, "There is no other hand!" But this type of preaching also undoubtedly risks provoking or enhancing division in a local congregation. Sometimes division may be necessary, but division should not be a normal pastoral goal. If a pastor wishes to preach about controversial issues but also wants to bring a congregation along gently, what, then, should he or she do? An approach developed in the congregational context by a career pastor is instructive.

Pastoral Preaching on Controversial Issues

Of the works cited above, Hamilton's was the most help for me in writing this chapter. The other books are written by seminary professors who also preach (though Wogaman left the seminary to serve a local church). Hamilton writes as a seminary-trained parish pastor. His grasp of the issues themselves is sophisticated, but his perspective is unashamedly pastoral. Though he doesn't spend a great deal of time on the theoretical aspects of what he does, he presents a kind of pragmatic pastoral ethics of dealing with controversies that I find to be very appealing.

Preliminaries

One of the most interesting of Hamilton's assertions from an ethical point of view is his opinion that a pastor should attempt to preach on controversial issues only after a relatively long tenure with a congregation.[7] He says that he wrote the sermons presented in his book only in his tenth year as pastor of that congregation, and he questions whether anyone should attempt to address such issues in the early years of a pastorate.

The astute reader will note that I had our fictional pastor Beth preach her capital-punishment sermon as she began her third year at St. Luke's. Conventional wisdom would assume that a pastor in his or her third year in a congregation is settling in, beginning to know the congregation and feel at home. That is true to a degree, but it is also true that the layers of people's lives are revealed to us only over time, as the flow of life brings them to light. Given Beth's tenure in her parish, we might ask, does she know whether anyone in her congregation has ever had a relative murdered or raped? Does she know if such cases have arisen in that community? Does she know whether someone in the congregation has a personal connection to a case involving a person about to be executed in her state? Most people's ethics are not formed theologically, as we preachers would like them to be, but rather develop out of their reactions to experiences in their lives.

Hamilton's assertion that people shouldn't preach about controversial issues till they have served a congregation a long time is reminiscent of homiletician Ron Allen's interpretation of Aristotelian rhetoric. In considering how people listen to sermons, Allen asserts that one of the three starting points from which people listen is that of *ethos*, which he defines as their relationship to the person speaking.[8] In essence, Hamilton is suggesting that it is the relationship of trust that allows people to hear and consider what you have to say about a topic, even if they disagree. Because they have built up over time a confidence that you will treat them fairly, they hear your arguments as fair, whether they like them or not.

Another key element in preaching on controversial issues is how you yourself approach the process. We go back to the pastoral principle of doing no harm. For this type of preaching, it is essential that you take the long view. Most people don't change their minds quickly or easily, certainly not as the result of a single sermon. It is important that the pastor see sermons such as this not as a final declaration of how the people must think (that, of course, would never work anyway), but rather as the beginning of an ongoing conversation. Indeed, one of the best ways to do this kind of sermon involves a formal invitation to dialogue. In some cases, for pastors who are confident of their ability to manage a public discussion well, that dialogue might even happen in the course of worship itself. Others might schedule a congregational luncheon and lead people in conversation around the tables afterward or set aside time on Sunday evening to hear responses from some designated members of the congregation and enter into general discussion. People respond much better if they hear you not as trying to dictate what they must think, but rather as offering them a place at the conversational table.

It is also important to remember that pastors do not have unlimited freedom when it comes to preaching on controversial issues. In some denominations the annual meeting or conference may adopt positions on issues to which pastors are then expected to adhere. For example, before the invasion of Iraq, the United Methodist Council of Bishops voted to oppose that invasion. A United Methodist pastor who chose to speak in favor of that invasion from the pulpit would know, at the very least, that she was opposing a position her supervisor would most likely hold. Denominations vary widely in the degree of uniformity of opinion they expect from their pastors. In a denomination that has high expectations for conformity, a wise pastor knows what that expectation is, keeps in mind the degree to which he or she is sworn to follow it, and goes against it only when absolutely necessary.

Hamilton asserts, and I agree, that it is essential to remember that issues are controversial precisely because they are complex.

"Because it is complex and multifaceted, a controversial issue by definition will result in multiple perspectives. An even more important assumption is that thinking, compassionate and caring people of faith can hold opposite positions on these issues."[9] A preacher who understands and accepts that equally devout members of the congregation may think differently and interpret the Bible differently with regard to an issue will be ready to preach in a way that respects those differences. A preacher who cannot accept that it is possible to consult the same Scriptures and come to opposite opinions on an issue will be much more likely to preach in ways that do harm to the unity of the congregation. This does not mean that a preacher cannot hold a strong and definite opinion on a given issue. It does mean that you as a preacher must keep in mind that an issue is about considerably more than what you may think about it.

Finally, choosing when to preach on a controversial issue depends on the situation. You will note that Beth chose to preach on capital punishment at a time when the congregation would be thinking about it anyway because of an upcoming execution in the state. Two distinct philosophies operate here. One is that this is precisely the time to preach on such an issue, because people will be thinking about it anyway. One important pastoral function is to help people deal with the challenges of life as they encounter them. The other philosophy is that controversial issues are best dealt with in the abstract, when nothing in the larger society is likely to inflame passions on the subject or keep people from listening objectively. According to this philosophy, you prepare them when the issue is not immediate, so that they can think through their response before they have to deal with it. My own sense is that a skillful pastor can make a real difference when an issue is current, provided that he or she is willing to follow certain canons of how to approach the sermon.

Preparing the Sermon

Study! Study! Study! It is essential that anyone who wants to preach on a controversial issue know the various positions that are commonly taken on the issue and why people hold those positions. In some cases your study will involve reading a considerable body of secular, perhaps even technical literature. You really can't decide on Monday that you plan to preach on stem-cell research this coming Sunday, unless you happen to be a cellular biologist with a ready knowledge of the literature. To treat such subjects casually, as though a half-informed opinion was good enough for the congregation, is to show a contempt for both your congregation and your profession.

It is also essential that we know the applicable scriptures and how they may be variously interpreted. People will want to know that you have done your biblical homework. It is especially important that you be ready to address passages that may appear to be in conflict or to lead to different conclusions on an issue. And it is important that you be clear in your own mind with regard to an interpretive principle by which you will evaluate apparent contradictions or differences. In my own tradition, for example, the 1963 Baptist Faith and Message Statement included in its paragraphs on the Scripture this closing sentence: "The criterion by which the Bible is to be interpreted is Jesus Christ." For me that sentence has become over the years a crucial interpretive template whenever the Bible appears to speak with more than one voice on an issue. When in doubt, I ask myself how I believe Jesus would approach the subject. That question invariably leads me to a fresh consideration of his life and witness that informs whatever decision I am trying to make. For me, for example, the critical principle with regard to the place of women in the church isn't anything Paul says on the subject. Paul says different things in different pastoral situations. For me the critical principle is how Jesus himself treated and valued the women he encountered in his ministry. Your tradition might point you to an interpretive principle different from mine, but knowing what sort of template you will use will help maintain consistency in your thinking.

It is important as well that we be acquainted with whatever creeds, confessions of faith, or statements of social policy our particular tradition may have in place on the issue. As I have suggested above, those statements may hold different degrees of authority for the preacher, but however they are used, it is important to know and understand what they say.

Once you have studied the material thoroughly and chosen a governing text for the day, you are ready to begin writing your sermon. Note that while this sort of sermon is unashamedly topical, I do not recommend departing from the practice of choosing a single primary text. It is especially tempting on some subjects to jump from scripture to scripture, attempting to develop whatever case we may be building. The problem is that such leapfrogging runs the serious risk of taking scripture passages out of context and thereby becoming vulnerable to misinterpretation. Scripture deserves to be treated more seriously than that. If you must use more than one text, make sure you take the time to interpret them properly as part of the sermon itself.

In a sermon on a controversial issue, the biblical text may enter into consideration at a later point than is usual for an ordinary sermon. Hamilton suggests that, when an issue has two distinct positions, the preacher proceed as follows: "I begin by presenting, as objectively and persuasively as possible, one position. About ten minutes into the sermon I then move to the second position. Again, I present this position with respect and passion."[10] By approaching the sermon this way, he creates an atmosphere in which people who disagree still feel that their position has been aired fairly as part of the presentation.

Some preachers, of course, find this very difficult to do. A preacher who believes one way on the abortion issue, for example, may find it nearly impossible to present the other side of the question fairly. *But that is precisely the point.* It is only by disciplining yourself to get inside the other side of the argument that you gain the ability to treat the folks who hold that position with the dignity and respect that everybody deserves. The more difficult this is for us to do as pastors, the more important it is that we do it. If it forces us, in order to preach on a topic, to walk down some streets we would prefer to avoid, that is part of the necessary journey of the pastorate. Only after he has done his best to present both sides fairly will Hamilton move to develop his own position on an issue.

Some issues have more than two sides. Others may not have crystallized into clearly opposing streams of thought. In these cases, the preacher's obligation is to help clarify the varying threads of the argument, so that people can better understand the issues. The temptation here is subtle: the temptation to shade ever so slightly the viewpoints with which we disagree by what we say or do not say. It is important to resist that temptation so as to keep our presentation scrupulously fair.

After the various sides of the argument have been presented, Hamilton moves to a statement of his own position. As a United Methodist pastor, he is careful to refer to any applicable statements from the United Methodist Church. He cites whatever data he believes to be important, and he brings in biblical texts that are his governing principles. His contention is that by taking this approach to the controversial sermon, he has created a space in which the congregation is able and willing to hear what he has to say about the issue. Even if they disagree with his conclusions, they know that he respects and understands their conclusions, and that assurance helps keep the discussion from becoming acrimonious.

Some people, of course, are not capable of tolerating preaching with which they disagree. Hamilton acknowledges that his church lost some members while he was preaching the series that was the occasion for his book.[11] You might lose members too. But you might gain others. Even if you do this kind of preaching very well indeed, you may still be criticized. But the call to preach is not the call to be timid. The key point here is that by taking an unashamedly and intentionally pastoral approach to preaching on controversial issues, Hamilton makes an ethical choice to put the welfare and unity of the congregation he serves first; at the same time, he helps members confront and examine those issues that typically divide people and congregations.

After the Sermon

As with the political issues we discussed in chapter 8, it is especially important that sermons on controversial issues not be limited to one-way conversation. Sometimes a preacher chooses to address a controversial issue not from the pulpit but rather in a seminar setting where responses and questions are built into the structure of the meeting. Sermons can be printed and made available for discussion in Sunday-school classes. With the Internet, you could post a sermon to the church's Web site and set up a chat room or threaded discussion that permits members to write out their questions and responses. Some people are much more comfortable communicating in writing than in person. That is why pastors get all those letters after an issues sermon! However you structure your follow-up, it is essential that you create an atmosphere in which church folk continue to believe that their opinions and feelings are understood and respected. That means you need to establish and encourage some clear means for communication. People will probably need to talk both with one another and with you about what they are thinking.

After the sermon, it is also important to maintain pastoral contact with those whom you know or believe disagree with you. People usually don't mind being disagreed with as long as those disagreements don't affect the relationship itself. The problem is that we pastors tend to assume that people don't want to talk with us when we disagree with them. If anything, the opposite is true. They may want to restate their arguments. They may want to ask questions about something we have said. Or they may simply need reassurance that the relationship is unharmed. In any case, this is a time for more pastoral contact, not less.

Finally, it is important to maintain that sense of modesty mentioned in earlier chapters as you prepare for, deliver, and deal with the aftermath of sermons on controversial issues. Hamilton observes at one point, "Finally, some of these issues will be impossible to resolve completely this side of eternity."[12] Just because you preached on a topic doesn't mean the discussion is over. Nor does it mean that things are settled in people's minds or that the church can move forward to concerted action on the issue. Change comes slowly in the church, and a pastor needs to realize and appreciate the organic quality of that growth. We plant seeds, we water, and we cultivate. We preach with the urgency of the gospel in and out of season. But real growth comes only in God's good time.

Notes

Chapter 1

1. Ronald D. Sisk, *The Competent Pastor: Skills and Self-knowledge for Serving Well* (Herndon, VA: Alban Institute, 2005), 3-20.
2. See, for example, Hans-Georg Gadamer, *Philosophical Hermeneutics* (Berkeley: University of California Press, 1976).
3. See John S. McClure, *Other-Wise Preaching: A Postmodern Ethic for Homiletics* (St. Louis: Chalice Press, 2001).
4. Thomas G. Long, *The Witness of Preaching*, 2nd ed. (Louisville: Westminster John Knox Press, 2005), 45-51.
5. Haddon W. Robinson, *Biblical Preaching: The Development and Delivery of Expository Messages*, 2nd ed. (Grand Rapids: Baker Academic, 2001), 31.

Chapter 2

1. Karl Barth, *Homiletics* (Louisville: Westminster John Knox Press, 1991), 81-82.
2. Thomas G. Long, *The Witness of Preaching*, 2nd ed. (Louisville: Westminster John Knox Press, 2005), 241.
3. Raymond H. Bailey, "Ethics in Preaching," *Review and Expositor* 86 (Fall 1989): 534.
4. Ibid.

Chapter 3

1. Ben J. Katt, *The Power of Persuasive Preaching* (St. Louis: Chalice Press, 2006).
2. Ibid., 41.
3. These concepts are treated in Ronald J. Allen, *Hearing the Sermon: Relationship, Content, Feeling* (St. Louis: Chalice Press, 2004).
4. Ibid., 18-41.
5. Ibid., 19.

Chapter 4

1. This chapter assumes an individual approach to planning worship. For a more communal approach that could help in dealing with some of these issues see Norma deWaal Malefyt and Howard Vanderwell, *Designing Worship Together: Models and Strategies for Worship Planning* (Herndon, VA: Alban, 2005).
2. See, for example, John R. Claypool, *Tracks of a Fellow Struggler: Living and Growing through Grief* (Waco, TX: Word Books, 1974), in which Claypool deals with the illness and death of his young daughter.
3. Malcolm Gladwell, *Blink! The Power of Thinking without Thinking* (New York: Little, Brown & Co., 2005).

Chapter 5

1. Leonora Tubbs Tisdale, *Preaching as Local Theology and Folk Art* (Minneapolis: Fortress Press, 1997), 60, quoted in Thomas G. Long, *The Witness of Preaching*, 2nd ed. (Louisville: Westminster John Knox Press, 2005), 65.
2. Ibid., 66.
3. See W. Jay Moon, "Using Proverbs to Contextualize Christianity in the Builsa Culture of Ghana, West Africa" (PhD diss., Asbury Theological Seminary, 2005), 156-7.

4. For more help in considering various cultural approaches to worship, see C. Michael Hawn, *One Bread, One Body: Exploring Cultural Diversity in Worship* (Herndon, VA: Alban, 2003).
5. See H. Richard Niebuhr, *Christ and Culture* (New York: Harper & Row, 1951).

Chapter 6

1. Diana Butler Bass, *Christianity for the Rest of Us: How the Neighborhood Church Is Transforming the Faith* (San Francisco: HarperSanFrancisco, 2006).

Chapter 7

1. Karl Barth, *Homiletics* (Louisville: Westminster John Knox Press, 1991), 85.
2. Ibid., 78.

Chapter 8

1. J. Philip Wogaman, *Speaking the Truth in Love: Prophetic Preaching to a Broken World*, (Louisville: Westminster John Knox Press), 1998, 58.
2. H. Richard Niebuhr, *Christ and Culture* (New York: Harper & Row, 1951). See especially Niebuhr's chapter on Christ transforming culture.
3. William H. Willimon, *Peculiar Speech: Preaching to the Baptized* (Grand Rapids: Eerdmans, 1992), 100.
4. John C. Bennett in *Handbook of Themes for Preaching*, James W. Cox, ed. (Louisville: Westminster John Knox Press, 1991), 44.
5. See Adam Hamilton, *Confronting the Controversies: A Christian Looks at the Tough Issues* (Nashville: Abingdon Press, 2001).

Chapter 9

1. From an exhortation by Father Zossima in Fyodor Dostoyevsky's 1879-1880 novel *The Brothers Karamazov*.
2. Abraham Lincoln, second inaugural address, quoted in Robert Kelley, *The Shaping of the American Past* (Englewood Cliffs, NJ: Prentice-Hall, 1975), 446.
3. For more help, see Kathleen S. Smith, *Stilling the Storm: Worship and Congregational Leadership in Difficult Times* (Herndon, VA: Alban, 2006).
4. Note that the preacher does not and cannot stand apart from what his or her people are experiencing in a crisis. The crisis has happened to us too. That means we must always be careful to be aware of and sensitive to our own feelings as we attempt to preach to others in these times.

Chapter 10

1. Adam Hamilton, *Confronting the Controversies: A Christian Looks at the Tough Issues* (Nashville: Abingdon Press, 2001).
2. J. Philip Wogaman, *Speaking the Truth in Love: Prophetic Preaching to a Broken World* (Louisville: Westminster John Knox Press, 1998).
3. Christine M. Smith, *Preaching as Weeping, Confession, and Resistance: Radical Responses to Radical Evil* (Louisville: Westminster John Knox Press, 1992).
4. Tony Campolo, *Is Jesus a Republican or a Democrat? And 14 Other Polarizing Issues* (Dallas: Word Publishing, 1995).
5. Smith, *Preaching as Weeping, Confession, and Resistance*, 2.
6. Ibid., 33.
7. Hamilton, *Confronting the Controversies*, 10.
8. Ronald J. Allen, *Hearing the Sermon: Relationship, Content, Feeling* (St. Louis: Chalice Press, 2004).
9. Hamilton, *Confronting the Controversies*, 11-12.
10. Ibid., 13.
11. Ibid., 10.
12. Ibid., 12.